HITHER & YON

hither & yon

A Travel Guide for the Spiritual Journey

Becca Stevens

Illustrations by Tara Armistead

DIMENSIONS
FOR LIVING
NASHVILLE

HITHER & YON
A TRAVEL GUIDE FOR THE SPIRITUAL JOURNEY

This book is printed on acid-free paper.

Library of Congress Cataloging-in-Publication Data
Stevens, Becca, 1963–
    Hither & Yon: a travel guide for the spiritual journey / Becca Stevens.
        p. cm.
    ISBN-13: 978-0-687-49076-9 (pbk. : alk. paper)
    1. Meditations.   2. Stevens, Becca, 1963–   .   I. Title.
    BV4832.3.S74 2005
    242—dc22

                                                                    2005015053

07 08 09 10 11 12 13 14 15 16—10 9 8 7 6 5 4 3 2 1
MANUFACTURED IN THE UNITED STATES OF AMERICA

To my husband, Marcus Hummon,
and our three sons, Levi, Caney, and Moses

A Place Called Hither and Yon

Hither and yon is a mysterious place of communion with God. It is the destination to which we are headed and the circuitous path itself. For the trip there are some things we should pack and some things we should leave behind. There are road signs to read and a language to cultivate. There are ways to walk, work, and pray. There are customs and practices that all respectful travelers need to observe. Hither and yon is the place that allows us to enter territories we never dreamed of in the world and in our hearts. We are already on the journey. This is written to encourage all of us to keep walking.

contents

acknowledgments

A SPECIAL THANK YOU TO JOE HOWARD FOR TEACHING ME HOW to walk in the woods; to Jack Fitzmier for helping me become a theologian; to Charlie Strobel for showing me how to live more compassionately; and to Cary Rayson, who shows us all how to keep preaching good news beyond our own brokenness.

A huge thank you to Carole Hagan for helping on the first edit of this book and to Angie Stephens, who typed most of this. To Susan, Donna, Regina, Jason, Ulea, Marlei, Peggy, Stacye, Holli, Kay, Sherri, Sheila, Mark, Toni, Sara, Connally, Angela, Leann, and all the employees of Thistle Farms.

Thanks to all the amazing volunteers at the Center for Contemplative Justice, Magdalene, and St. Augustine's Chapel, including Carlana, John, Bonnie, Melissa, Gordon, Mark, Lyn, Dick, Allen, Michael, Jeanne, Tori, Jodi, Rod, Gilbert, Rick, Peggy, Russ, Matraca, Mary Jane, Sigourney, Gene, Orrin, Anna, Camilla, Holly, Kacky, Katrina, Marti, John, Lyn, Todd, Margaret, June, Marshall, Mary, Rick, Tara, Keith, Judy, Doug, Gay, and hundreds of others who keep those programs thriving.

I am grateful every day for the lessons from patient teachers and for meaningful work. This community is living testimony to how beautiful love can be.

introduction

Jesus told his disciples, "Take neither purse nor belt for the journey" (Mark 6:8).

I HAVE LONGED FOR GOD MY WHOLE LIFE. SOMETIMES THAT longing gives me an acute passion for following what I think of as my calling. But sometimes it feels like an unrequited love.

I remember sitting in a seminary class as the professor was talking about baptisms. I felt my heart pumping blood and could feel a burning sensation in my fingers and toes. I thought about how the professor was casually talking about offering our children back to God, and I still hadn't figured out how to offer myself to God. I knew sitting there that my feelings were being distilled into a promise that even if I never felt love fulfilled, I was willing to walk toward God with no regret for the rest of my life. And that has been my ministry.

That walk by its nature has been filled with longing. It has not been lonely, though, as there have been many people along the way who have reflected God's love. For years I prayed that my longing would be healed so that I would feel more settled in my faith. There is a tendency in our prayer life to pray for what we think is missing, believing that what we lack is what we need. What I discovered was that many times what is lacking is the gift itself. One day I was praying in a beautiful new temple. It had been designed so that the entire front wall was etched glass. As I studied the glass, I realized that it was the scratches in the glass that made it beautiful. The longing was what etched my soul. The longing was the gift to carry with me on the journey. It would keep me close to my faith. Longing is the place from which I look out into the world.

When I meet a woman walking the streets who uses drugs and sex to numb herself, I swear that I recognize another human trying to fill deeper scratches and longings than I may ever know. When I sit with a person who has dismissed most of faith and Scripture, I see a fellow pilgrim longing to believe some truth about God. When I talk to a student who asks if I think you have to be Christian to go to heaven, I see a child searching for a compassionate creator who would never abandon one of her own.

All this leads me right here. I want to write about the thoughts, people, and experiences that have led me hither and yon and back to be with God. The road has carried me around the world and into the shadowed parts of my heart. I still have a long distance to cover; but in the midst of the journey, I am ready to put language to the feelings and thoughts and to remind others that there are ways to travel in the world that carry us to far-off places, allow us to live lavishly in love, and enable us to see the richness of poverty, the extravagance of a foot-washing, the tenderness of human touch.

For me, hither and yon represents the destination and the journey. It is the ideal of traveling free, to be in the reach of God everywhere. It is not something to be gained; it is simply experienced every now and then by the grace of God. It is not to be planned; it is simply being open to visions when God allows the clouds to part. It is not certain; it is just remembering that God has given us all we need to make this journey. Traveling to hither and yon is a spiritual discipline without strict practices. It is more faith than theology, more coincidence than ritual. In the end we are just servants doing our duty as best we can.

Our journey begins with God and carries us back to God. Longing for God is part of the experience. Ultimately all roads lead back to the heart, even in death. Whatever happens to me when I leave my body is a wonderful mystery. My prayer is that I will have enough courage to dive into that mystery when the time comes and trust that part of the journey. I still hold out hope for the ideal of heaven. In the place of consciousness on the eternal side of time, I pray that I will know what it is to have that love requited.

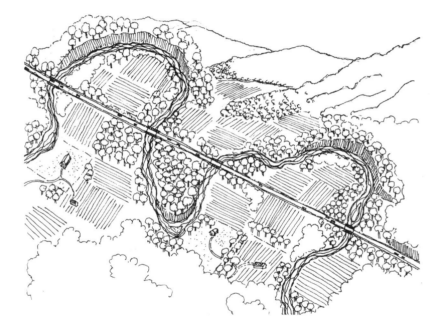

1. planning the journey

Burning My Purse

I carry from my past
A silken purse bound to my waist,
Holding silver coins and pearls
Traded for my innocence.

I wish a moth would eat through it
Or a thief cut me loose.
I can't lay such riches down
Or let it go to forgiveness.

I want to offer it as a sacrifice,
Lay it all on the altar of my youth,
Confess stories as the pearls roll out,
Then burn it as a sign of my penance.

I would dance around the flame,
Marvel at my unbridled heart,
Done grieving things I can't change,
And holding onto useless treasure.

IT BEGINS WITH A THOUGHT

THERE IS A MYSTERIOUS SPACE SOMEWHERE BETWEEN HEAD and heart, intellect and soul. It is a place of imagination and of prayer. It is a place where muses live and visions begin. If we could see thoughts born there, they might attach themselves to a breath and float into the air like a buzzard in an upward draft. The thoughts circle around our heads until gravity pulls them down to the ground, and there they are laid to rest.

Other thoughts born there might float out beyond gravity. As these thoughts rise into the sky, they might look more like a kite tail. They wave in the wind and move toward the heavens. Floating freely, they aren't dragged down by reason or doubt. Eventually, like the kite tail, they become so small and distant that they are simply lost in the oblivion of space, swallowed up by the universe. They have no impact; they just disappear.

But every now and then a thought, born in that space between head and heart, takes on dimension and weight. It doesn't move like a kite tail; it is more like a shooting star. It feels different. It has purpose and weight and pushes things out of the way to make room for itself. This mysterious thought travels, not into oblivion, but into the fabric of creation. It sits with God, right in God's bosom, and has a place. This is the place of hither and yon where, every now and then, we can visit. It is not here or there; it isn't inside or outside our bodies. We can't really put a finger on it. It is a place we are privileged to see and to taste in small bites. Humanity was created to commune with this place, and we have been traveling there since original grace.

One time when I was twenty-three years old, I was lost in the Kalahari Desert. I had traveled with a young woman from Botswana who thought she could take me across the Kalahari into Namibia. She was as lost as I was; and, through a combination of bad luck and funny coincidence, we ended up stranded about eighty miles into the desert. We had an entire afternoon to sit under one shade tree and think. I thought about all the roads that had led to that sandy path that was trickling into oblivion in front of me. It was almost funny, except that I felt completely lost and exposed. I had no idea where my Botswanan friend and I were or how we could get out and neither did she. So, with no other choice, we just let everything go; and we sat.

We sat and sat and didn't even talk after awhile. I kept thinking about the desert fathers and why they must have gone out to the desert. They went there because, when there is nothing else, God fills the space. My only stumbling block to being completely lost in prayer and love was that I couldn't get past worrying for my own safety.

Finally, about six hours later, just as the sun was beginning to turn orange and hang near the horizon, a nomadic bush group appeared. They took us in, fed us with no questions or judgment, and gave us animal skins sewn together for bedding. The next day a medical truck gave us a ride to a town close to Namibia.

I have spent the last fifteen years trying to get back to that desert where there is nothing else but God. Only this time I would like to return with no fear. I think that was one of the first times I saw that the way I traveled in the world could be part of the interior journey toward God, in a mysterious world as infinite as the Kalahari Desert. Infinity goes both ways. It is possible to dissect an inch forever, into infinitesimal amounts. And so it is possible to believe that a single thought dreamt in the deepest part of us, a place between head and heart, space and time, hither and yon, can have infinite qualities. A thought in the middle of an African desert can be my connection to the eternal.

It is miraculous to me to believe that with our finite and fearful bodies, we can birth thoughts of infinite proportions. It means we are eternal in our spirits and more than flesh and bone. It means we need to honor one another and make sure that space is sacred. It means I need to respect your thoughts. It means when we worship, we are giving ourselves permission to imagine, dream, pray, and commune with God from a place within ourselves.

THE ETERNAL TIMELINE

IT TAKES LESS THAN A MOMENT TO GET TO HITHER AND YON,
but we spend our whole lives making our way there. The
best way to get there is to give up thinking about linear
time. The mantra "It's the journey and not the destination" is applicable.

There was a mystic who prayed constantly for visions.
After years of praying, he saw an illumined, wooded
meadow and realized that he was in the presence of God.
As the moment passed, he awoke aching for the vision to
return. He said that it was humbling to wait for that
moment of communion for so long and then to have it
pass so quickly. He spent the next few years praying to
return to that place of union with God.

Many faithful pilgrims spend their lives in the work of
prayer and meditation and love of their neighbors. Some
talk of longing for years to hear God's voice. A few speak
of the absence of God for years. And one speaks of the
fear of God's forsaking him just before his death. It will
take our whole lives to see where the journey is headed,
and so in the meantime we fill it with right actions and
spiritual disciplines that make the traveling lighter.

In hither and yon, time is not a constant. It is relative,
depending on where we are standing on the timeline of

life. Imagine for a moment a long line segment stretched out. The first point on the line is the moment of our birth; the last point is the time of our death. All the points in between are markers—for birthdays, significant events, tragic losses, major decisions. There is a point for this moment. The points around this moment seem to have more space between them than the points ten years ago. The points that make up this day seem to take longer than imagined points on a similar day five years ago. In fact, most of the points five years ago have blurred together into a single point. Points farther out into the future seem almost impossible to reach. But what if from this present point we can see no others? What if there isn't a line at all—just a dot that is this moment? We can stand on it, completely content that we are not moving forward or backward. We are just resting on a point that is the representation of our lives.

That point is the eternal moment; and if we choose to, we can live in that moment. That is the point I am seeking. Even as I am driving my kids to school and typing these words on a screen, I am trying to stay on the point. The invitation of hither and yon is to stay on the point and fill the moment, knowing that we are standing with God and that is enough.

THE MAP

IF I HAD TO DRAW A MAP OF THE PATH TO GOD, I THINK IT
would look like the Caney Fork River in Middle
Tennessee. Driving I-40 East from Nashville to
Crossville, you cross the river no less than five times.
A map of the river would look like a long, squiggly line.
You cross it, and two miles later there is a sign announcing that you are crossing it again. This happens several
more times before you realize just how circuitous a path
the river travels.

Sometimes when I am not rushed, I wish I were on the
river instead of the interstate. The interstate has been
there only for about forty years, but the river seems to
have been around forever. It has taken its time cutting the
path and has gradually learned that wandering is a good
thing. The river knows that this path is how its banks were
built and how the fish thrive. This path keeps the land
around it from being destroyed and is the way to get to
deeper waters. On our spiritual map, the river's meander-
ings back and forth can be seen as markers along the way.

The first time you approach one of the river-crossing
markers, it comes almost out of the blue. You are traveling along the interstate when the terrain drops; and suddenly you are driving over a beautiful river steeped in

lush green and headed for a hillside, until it bends and disappears. This first crossing reminds us to find ourselves. This is the place to begin hearing our voice. It is the voice, either nurtured or silenced by others, that is unique in the world. It is the voice we've known, but still it startles us to hear it. Thank God for this voice that will give us direction on the journey. Thank God that it pulls us to listen to our hearts and to be connected to the Spirit.

It is good to find ourselves; but then we must lose ourselves again, and that is what the second crossing tells us. It is important to get lost and question where we are and where we are headed. It is a great gift to lose ourselves literally and to remember that we can't claim the truth, which we only glimpse through cloudy skies. I heard someone say at the end of a worship service to "get up, get out, and get lost." Being lost means we are willing to admit we are not sure what's around the bend, but we still trust the Spirit. Being lost means we need other people and are in need of prayer.

When the river crosses the road a third time, it calls us to forget ourselves completely. There is nothing worse than a spiritual pilgrim who is self-absorbed. This is the time to learn that it is not just about us; it is about all God's children. We are neither found nor lost. We are to love and tend to the suffering in the world. This teaching was synthesized for us in a listing of the corporeal acts of mercy in the thirteenth century: Feed the hungry, clothe the naked, give drink to the thirsty, tend the sick, comfort the sorrowful, visit the prisoners, and bury the dead. That is the way of the river. Those of us on its path take a long time to arrive, because we can't make the spiritual journey as the crow flies. We stop along the way to help a brother or sister in need. We forget about our own journey and love our neighbor. This marker on the crossing, where the river seems headed completely in the wrong direction, is what keeps us focused on the work. It doesn't feel like an easy path, and it is not endearing to people who need a quick spiritual fix.

Once we have been given the grace to find, lose, and forget ourselves, the fourth crossing calls us to remember ourselves. I take this phrase almost literally: We are supposed to "re-member" ourselves, to put ourselves back together. We know ourselves again in the context of being God's beloved children. We remember that we were created in the image of love and feel that the worth of our lives comes from the Creator. This marker feels like a great gift and joy on the walk. I love experiencing myself in the context of a community, grounded in a God who loves all creation. I think this marker keeps me going when sometimes I become afraid and wake up thinking, *What have I been doing? How did I get here?*

Several months ago, while speaking to a group of young men in prison about women on the streets, I ended up talking for thirty minutes about love. I said that love is the most radical way we can change the world and that it can filter through the judicial system into the prison and change all our hearts. Just as I was saying this, I woke up to myself and looked at the mostly young black men who were being kind and patient with me. Suddenly I remembered myself and almost started crying. I could see clearly that racism filtering through all the systems is as American as apple pie and as entrenched in our nation as the stars and stripes. I could see poverty as deep as any river in America, keeping all the systems flowing; and for just a minute I could see my part in it. It is in moments such as these that we remember who we are and why we need to be traveling with God's mercy.

When the river crosses for the fifth time, the marker is inviting us to love ourselves. We have heard the call of amazing grace and found that, in the crossing, God's grace always calls us back to love. Standing in the circle of prisoners after that talk, a young man gave me the number of a woman who needed my help. He said he knew the Spirit had brought me there so that his friend could get help. I don't know if the Spirit will ever bring our paths together again; but if we both meander around the streets long enough, I bet it will.

Crossing the Caney Fork River only takes us a fraction of an inch across the map of America. There are always other rivers to cross and mountains to climb.

THE LEGEND

EVERY MAP HAS A LEGEND TO HELP US FIND OUR WAY ON THE journey. The world is full of signs and symbols that are there for our spiritual divining.

Once, while working at a storefront homeless shelter and trying to decide if I could get ordained, I met a priest who said that when you're making a decision, pray for a sign and keep going. It has been good advice. It means we should not be stopped in our tracks by indecision or inability to discern God's voice, but it also means we must not rush forward without any direction or insight into our lives. It means we keep working and loving our neighbor while at the same time watching and praying.

The map legend is different for everyone, but signs are given to all of us. They are the symbols and events that call us into God's presence. They remind us that God is present, that there is more to this world than we can explain, and that all of creation can speak to us about our lives.

It takes years of practice to read the legend. It seems almost impossible at times. The grace is in the joy we feel every time we learn a new symbol or sign. Hearing the birds and praying next to an old sycamore tree helps. It also helps to be silent and take in our surroundings.

Once when I was praying with my child at night, he said, "Mom, be quiet. I can't hear." It is in the silence that prophets hear the voice of God. Legends show us the possibilities of leaving what is familiar in order to find a new path as we make our way in the world.

Signs and symbols also appear in the noisy, mundane routine of our lives. If we wait to sit cross-legged on a mountaintop in silence before seeing a vision, we may miss the sign that pops up in the grocery store. Walking down the streets of New York City, one can be washed in noise and still hear God's call: garbage collectors rolling a trash cart with small wheels down the cracked-filled sidewalk right behind me; cabs and drivers, stopping and starting, all trying to find the path the crow would fly; music from a street player; people talking into the air on phones; the sound of shoes on the curb. In the midst of the noise of our lives, it takes discipline to recognize God speaking to us about humility, humanity, compassion, and patience.

Learning to read the legend means that we don't wait for a diamond; we look at the quartz in pebbles. We don't wait for a rare blue rose; we look at wildflowers growing in the grass next to the prison fence. When we get to be experts, we can even recognize God's mercy in the pebbles and the fence.

The downside of looking for signs is that it can make us a little superstitious. My mom has been dead for nine years, and I miss her still. I miss having her see my incredible children and being proud of me when I make a cake for no special reason. I wish I could have shown her my first book and the part about her funeral being a wonderful tribute to her life. So instead I water a plant that someone gave me when she died. It is a peace lily, and they just don't die. At least it hasn't died for nine years even though it has come close a couple of times. One morning I decided it was time to plant it outside. I thought it needed a break from indoor living, and the soil was about gone. I held a ritual to thank the plant for connecting me to my mother, for staying alive, and for forgiving me the times I neglected it. I carried the root ball to the side door. When I opened the door, lodged between the door and the screen was a dead bird. I called to my husband, "Marcus, come down here. There is a dead bird in the house." My husband came because he could tell my voice was a little shaky. It was as though I had walked under a ladder or spilled salt or broken a mirror. There is a lesser-known old adage that if a bird dies in your house, someone close to you will die. I wish I didn't know it, and I certainly don't believe it; but it did frighten me. Besides, I was in the middle of burying a plant. "It's not in the house," my husband pointed out to me. "It's just almost in the house."

It is all so silly. It's silly to think this plant is connected to my mother. It's silly to see a dead bird and worry for everyone I love. It's silly to believe any of it, but maybe the saving grace is that all the silliness leads me to prayer. Then prayer leads me to God.

The point of the legend is learning to see the world as sacred and to understand how we are part of creation. That ongoing lesson is theology in its truest sense. It is the study of God. It is watching the world, listening to conversations with an open heart, paying attention to thoughts that just seem to rise up, being open to signs. Even though we cannot always read all the signs, it doesn't stop us from contemplating their marvels and rejoicing in their presence.

helpful hints

- All of us are born with everything we need to make the journey. Everyone can see visions: Visions are sight filled with grace. Everyone is a mystic: Mystics are people who see visions and are willing to bear witness to them. Everyone is a prophet: Prophets are people who are willing to speak the truth of their visions to the world.

- It's good to be a little suspicious about institutions and rituals. I have learned that all institutions, religious or otherwise, are willing to sacrifice their own to keep their marketshare. The way to remain standing is to be humble in religious arguments and fierce in defending the underdog. Even if we have been walking into the same office for years, we need to keep looking at our surroundings with some skepticism.

- In seeking hither and yon, don't settle for less. Hither and yon is the place where we go beyond the rituals, behind the scrims, and beneath the altars in the Holy of the Holies. It is the place where all the possessions and positions we hold onto collapse in on themselves. It is the place where religious leaders are brought to their knees and where the oppressed learn to stand.

When we arrive, we will feel blessed and may begin to understand why Moses took off his shoes near the burning bush.

A Prayer for the Journey

God, set me on the path again.
Turn me to the rising sun
*   when I need to be inspired.*
Turn me to wilderness
*   when I need to be lost.*
Turn me toward the business of the world
*   when I need to work.*
Turn me toward the mountain
*   when I need to be refreshed.*
Then turn me toward the sunset
*   when I need rest.*
Amen.

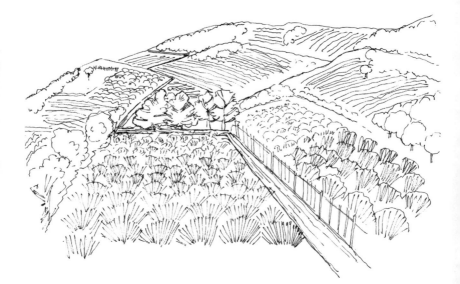

2. preparing to travel

Sitting With My Thoughts

I am happy sitting with my thoughts.
They are rich company.
Memories, like flowered wallpapers,
Hung when time was slower,
Decorate my interior halls.
Fading makes them sweeter,
The aging more tender.
Desire, like decanted brandy,
Sits on interior shelves.
Knowing it's there, capped,
Makes my throat burn.

Travel is easy in this space,
Where dreams are free to take time.
Thoughts, beyond words, live in wind,
And carry me quicker than smell
To sacred ground I once walked.

HEAD TOWARD THE FEAR

ON THE SPIRITUAL JOURNEY, FOLLOW THE FEAR. AND WHEN you bump into it, know that it is a good place to stop and take stock.

Fear lives in all of us and tries to keep us separated from love. I always believed that we could move through fear to get to love, but I have discovered that it doesn't work that way. I can't will myself to overcome fear or surrender to it, thinking it will pass. It will crop up in the middle of the night or visit me in my weakness. If I don't try to avoid fear, it can serve as a reality check on my mortality. It can become part of my life and can teach me about needing others, learning from others, and being grateful for the moment. When I head toward fear and accept it with love, eventually my fear will move out of love's way. This may sound paradoxical, but I believe it to be true.

We don't have to surrender to our fear; we surrender to love, and love will move our fears aside. We can trust that fear will walk with us on the path and that it will offer us many gifts. We can also trust that love is more powerful than fear and ultimately that love will find us on the path and clear the way.

This does not mean that we should risk our peace of mind or safety to seek out fears for no reason. It doesn't mean that we should try risky physical and mental challenges to prove our courage and challenge love. It just means that staying safe and secure within our comfort zone closes our borders and doesn't expand our love into the world.

Everyone's comfort zone is different, and so we will have to decide for ourselves where to draw our boundaries and how to expand them for the sake of loving more. I know this doesn't sound helpful. We would rather be told, "Go east four miles, and turn right by the old sycamore tree." Actually, though, this advice is similar. What we can do is pray, meditate, walk, work, and sleep with our hearts open to the idea of God's calling. Then, when we reach a place where we are afraid to go, that's where we should turn right and stay awhile. It's holy ground, where we are called to lay aside our fears for love.

One of my fears since childhood was dying. My father died in an accident when I was young and was buried within twenty-four hours of his death. As a little girl I kept wondering if they were sure he was dead. Maybe he would have gotten better after a couple of days and would have awakened before he was buried. I even had a recurring nightmare as a child that I was still alive at my funeral, but as an adult I have chosen a profession in which I can't avoid dealing with death. I am so grateful that I have been given the opportunity to head into this fear and find God's loving presence sitting by a deathbed, healing hearts at funerals, calling communities together in grief, and helping me understand that we are put on this earth to prepare to die. If I had not been able to walk through the fear, there would be so much love I would have missed.

Over the years as a priest, I know that my fear of death has actually helped me to be more loving and pastoral when faced with the death of others. If I can believe that love is stronger than my fear, then I can trust the journey and be attentive and compassionate at a deathbed. I can listen with my whole heart and mind to the person dying and to the family. When I was a chaplain in training at the veterans' hospital, I was assigned to the cancer ward. It was really scary for me at first. I thought, *I can't do this. I can't sit and watch someone die. It's just too hard.*

What I learned during the internship was that I could. I could sit there for hours, and in the end I could feel God's love and compassion. I sat with men easily my father's age, many of whom had little or no family visiting them. I would sit there and listen to their fears, hear their stories about their children, and offer them a hand and an honest prayer for their peace and joy.

CLEANING HOUSE

"GIVE AWAY WHAT YOU THINK YOU CAN'T LIVE WITHOUT."

I remember those words coming from a nun who was staying at our house. I heard her speak the words so clearly that I have never doubted their truth for a moment, but I haven't lived them. By God's grace, I have lost or have had stolen most of the possessions I probably would have clung to if left to my own devices.

One gift of my inability to hang on to things is that my family doesn't have a key to our house. The door is always open. Though we have had three cars stolen from the driveway, no one has ever entered the house unless invited. I think the reason is that people are always around. We have home church every week, and our children have friends over all the time to skateboard or play. My husband writes most of his music in our front room, and people are meeting and working around the house almost every day. The unplanned result is that community has replaced the security system. Whatever we have in our house is shared with anyone who walks through the door.

I still have much cleaning to do, metaphorically and literally. I live out of old injuries that make me want to build closets with thoughts or memories and then shut them tight, and so I keep going back into my life and heart to throw out things that do me no good. We have to clean out that which keeps our hands clenched with the fear that it can be taken. When our hands are clenched, they aren't open to the world. Think about running into a homeless man on the street. There are a million possible reactions and no single right response. The right response is the one not chosen out of guilt, fear, ignorance, or clinging to what we think is ours. The right response comes from compassion, love, generosity, and the knowledge that genuine help is possible. On a spiritual walk, nothing that we have is ours. All is God's to be shared.

I walked down the street with a man who has worked with just about every chronically homeless man in the city. He was approached in the parking lot by a stranger who began to talk, and my friend took a minute to listen. He has probably heard more stories—lies and truths—from people needing help than any person I have ever met. Yet, he took sixty seconds to listen. He responded to the man; and we parted ways. I remember the meeting as humane and dignified. If we head out on our journey before cleaning house, we may feel threatened by such encounters. After we clean, we have reserves to offer others.

In the Gospel of John, Jesus began his journey by cleaning out the Temple. He went into the center of spiritual worship in Jerusalem and cleaned out all that was not God's. It was a brave and wise beginning, an example of how to start; but it is much harder to do than it sounds.

There are many reasons for us to shy away from cleaning out our hearts, homes, and sacred spaces. First, our temple is filled with all that is familiar. It is comforting to live with what we know. The furniture is worn by the way we like to sit. We have memorized the words in the liturgy. We know what it is to live with the familiar feelings of our hearts. To clean out all of that means things would look different. It means there would be awkward silences and empty spaces. It is difficult to clean out the old when we have no idea what will replace it. Second, the Temple is beautiful. It was made with polished stone, hand-carved wood, and carpets woven by a community of women. The old closets of our hearts are lined with memories and polished over many years into images and stories. Third, if we clean the temple, what will be left to fill the space? It is frightening to imagine that we could clean it all out.

If we sweep the basement, clear the cobwebs, and give away the store, we may be left empty-handed; but would that be so bad? The promise is in the cleaning. We are left with a sense of freedom and excitement. When we clean the house, we find new spaces and notice light dancing in places where we didn't know it shone. We are literally and spiritually lighter. When we clean out old resentments, revenge is gone and grudges are dumped. It is not that we can't cherish the old; it is that the old shouldn't make it impossible to experience the new.

I remember the story of my father's coat. He was a young priest serving a congregation and trying to feed the family. My mother had just given him a new overcoat for Christmas to replace his well-worn, threadbare coat. He wore the old coat for casual events and saved his new coat for important events. He was a two-coat man, always protected from the cold winters of Connecticut. Our house was close to the railroad tracks; and so it wasn't unusual when the day after Christmas a man hopped off a train, shivering, and knocked on our front door. We listened as our father answered the knock. We heard the murmur of voices. The next sounds were of the closet door opening, then shutting. Finally the front door closed, and my father returned to our family. My mom said, "You gave that man the old coat, didn't you?" "No," my father replied. "I gave him the new coat." That story has fed me for years. It makes me joyful and proud of him, and I try to emulate his generosity.

PACKING LIGHT

IT SEEMS APPROPRIATE THAT WHILE WRITING THIS BOOK I HAVE not had an office or a pulpit of my own. I have been transcribing and editing at borrowed desks and in coffee shops on the way to meetings. Because of it, I don't carry much around.

The congregation that I have served for the past eleven years, St. Augustine's Chapel at Vanderbilt University, has been thriving and growing; and so we launched a capital campaign to build a new center for contemplative justice. We moved out of our worship space over a year ago so the renovations could begin. We eagerly looked forward to having a building that would meet codes and would allow for people with disabilities to participate fully; but politics intervened, and the renovations have taken longer than expected. We worship and work in borrowed spaces on the campus and at other churches. Each Sunday morning, a few of us unpack a big plastic trunk that holds our "church" and afterward pack it away. On the outside of the trunk are the words *St. Augustine's Chapel*. We have reduced what once occupied over five thousand square feet into a trunk that we can carry around. It is a beautiful gift.

When the disciples headed out, they were told to take a staff but no belt or purse and only one pair of shoes. That is packing light, and it makes the most sense if we can live in community. Packing light means that we rely on other people to help meet our daily needs.

A couple of years ago, I led a group of twenty-five people on a journey to Ecuador. Upon unpacking the first night, I discovered that I had forgotten my clothes. I had brought books, bedding, and costumes for the children's play but no clothes. At first I panicked, but then I asked the group for help. I couldn't believe the response. People offered me new underwear, a batik skirt, and t-shirts that had been bought just for the trip. I had clothing all week and felt grateful. I looked nicer than if I had packed my old things. It is a blessing to be in need and to experience the generosity of others.

Packing light doesn't mean you simply take enough for yourself; it means that you don't worry about having everything you need, and you pack with others in mind. During the trip to Ecuador I was still able to share plenty out of my bags with everyone. I had tons of sunblock and treats.

The point is to give not out of obligation but out of a sense of joy. The joy is that you can offer some tiny bit of what God and others have given you your whole life. This is the message of the good Samaritan. The story has been preached a thousand times, and often the pastor tells the congregation that we must be more like the Samaritan than the Levite or the priest. I think we forget that often we are the person in the ditch and that we need to be thankful when someone carries us to a safe place.

That lesson has been preached to me a thousand times by the women of Magdalene, a residential community for women who have a criminal history of prostitution and drug abuse. I have witnessed women literally walk off the streets with nothing to their names, not even a change of clothes, but with the promise that while they begin to heal, our community will take care of their needs. With complete and utter faith, they come with us. They don't have a purse or two pairs of sandals; they just want help. Once in a Magdalene house, having had rest and time to reflect, the women say that love in the form of a house key or a new bedspread is a sign of God's mercy. When we are given the gift of witnessing this in someone else's life, it takes us to our knees in gratitude.

One benefit of packing light is that there is room in our bags for something new. I knew a couple who had been married for almost thirty years. The husband was diagnosed with cancer, and for several weeks he had to be in the hospital. When I went to visit and asked how they were doing, they both said, "Great." The wife explained they had been carrying around a great deal of old baggage for years. It was heavy, but neither one of them could put it down. When the husband became so sick that they had to check into the hospital, the wife said there wasn't room for the baggage. It didn't fit, so they had to leave it outside the hospital door. They forgave each other everything and were freer than they had been in years. What a blessing it would be to give ourselves that gift, not just at the end of our journey but all the way through. What a joy it would be to leave our old baggage at the door and to walk straight and free.

In order to pack light, we have to believe that our needs can be swallowed up in God's abundance. Early one Monday morning not too long ago, I sat fretting in my office. The summer months always translate into financial stress for nonprofit organizations, and the money in the accounts for the five houses of Magdalene was only enough for six weeks. I was looking at the books, wondering where we would acquire enough money to carry us into fall. Just then, the woman who makes our deposits entered and knelt by the safe to roll the tumblers and open it. Jokingly I said, "You need to lay hands on the safe before you open it." She smiled and said, "Haven't you ever heard of the loaves and fishes?" The irony was that this story was the gospel I was preparing to preach, and it had never occurred to me that I had to apply it to my own scarcity. I knew I needed to address the context of the gospel story, to emphasize that it is told six times, and to try to inspire people with the proclamation that God fills our hunger. What I had forgotten was that I had to do that in faith myself.

I once heard that there is enough food in the world to feed all the hungry children. It is not a lack of resources; it is simply a lack of will. When I think about what I have hoarded or held onto because of fear, it causes me great grief. I want to walk, eat, pack, and work with an open and trusting heart.

WHAT TO WEAR

THERE IS NO REASON TO WORRY ABOUT DRESS. SACRED TEXTS tell us not to worry about what to wear. On the journey that is inward and outward, the idea is not to let clothing get in the way; but that may not be as easy as it sounds.

Once my brother said, "You actually can judge a book by its cover." We all laughed, but in a way he was right. We would never get anything accomplished if we didn't judge some books by their covers, make a decision to read them or not, and then move on. In terms of clothing, this means that we shouldn't let what we wear misrepresent us to ourselves or others. Our clothing should reflect what is of value to us in our lives.

I admit that I do not have this part down. My clothes trip me up sometimes. Since I am an Episcopal priest, I am expected to wear a black shirt with a clerical collar. For the life of me, I can't wear it; but I can't quite figure out how to dress appropriately without it. If someone judges my cover, they might say that I am a little disrespectful and a bit sloppy. In spite of my struggles with this aspect of my life, what I'm clear about is that our cover should not preoccupy our minds. What to wear should not occupy much time, talent, or treasure. We should just wear what's accessible and clean and keep going.

Many traditions have special clothing for rituals, which eliminates the problem of having to worry about how to dress. The pilgrims to Mecca wear white for purification. When spiritual leaders are conducting services, they often wear vestments in order not to distract people by their clothing. In many Christian traditions, the faithful wear white three times: At baptisms, white represents new life; at weddings, white represents purity; at funerals, white symbolizes resurrection. The clothing becomes part of the symbolism in all three rituals.

On our journey, we would do well to follow the mantra "less is more"; and that is certainly true for clothing. We don't need much. The more we care for our bodies beneath the wrapping, the more we will easily wear whatever clothes we choose. If we are rested, are at peace, and have tended to body and spirit, then we will look at home in our clothing. If we are trying to look rested and peaceful but really aren't, then it's all just a style and doesn't have meaning. Consider the lilies of the field as Jesus advised in Matthew 6, and then decide how important it is whether you have straight or flared legs on your jeans.

Though we are packing light, there's one item we might want to consider taking: beatific lenses. These are lenses that help us see the world not simplistically or unrealistically but as sacred. These are the lenses of the Beatitudes that help us see God's presence in everything.

Using these lenses doesn't mean that there is no suffering; it just means we see God in the suffering.

Once a woman named Hilda was dying. She told me her only prayer was not to return to the hospital before she died because she didn't think she could handle it. The next day, she was taken back to the hospital. When I drove to visit, I was worried about how disappointed and sad she was going to be. When I arrived, Hilda said she was fine. She said she had forgotten that God was in the hospital and that God was close by as she was preparing to die. It was humbling, and I will never forget her witness to the rest of us who are traveling.

It doesn't matter where we go or what we wear. God will be there. Our job is not to bring God to a place; our job is to recognize God wherever we find ourselves. God finds us in the most unexpected places and allows us to find peace.

WHAT TO EAT

FAITH TRADITIONS HAVE SO MANY RULES ABOUT EATING THAT I couldn't possibly list them all. To me, the main point is to make sure that food and drink are part of our lives in a way that allows us to travel well. If they become a problem, we will know it better than anyone else.

There are times for feasting and times for fasting, and knowing the difference requires us to pay attention to our bodies and the seasons of our lives. I tend to think there are more people who like to feast than to fast. I would encourage all who like the feast to be about the fast as well, perhaps during the seasons that world faiths set aside for fasting. I have always liked Advent (the four weeks before Christmas) and Lent (the forty days before Easter) much more than the actual feasts. These seasons of fasting are times for inner reflection, and there are no gifts to purchase. Ramadan and Yom Kippur offer more opportunities for fasting.

The reason that fasting has remained part of the spiritual journey for thousands of years is that it works. When we stop eating for a day—or several days, if we can manage it—our minds, bodies, and spirits are cleared and we gain a new perspective on the world. Once, a group of about two hundred of us were fasting with special intention for all who suffered without health care. On the second day,

I started feeling a little euphoric. I was feeling compassion and renewed energy. When I awoke on the third day, I wasn't hungry. I had made it over the hump and wanted to go to the woods to pray for everyone. I knew that my fast was a pittance of an offering, but I felt I was fasting with the best intentions. I realize that many of us who fast as a spiritual discipline will never know real hunger, but we can glimpse what it means to empty ourselves and know the Spirit better.

The food we eat is an essential part of our rituals and becomes symbolic of God's presence. At a Seder, everything we eat is symbolic of Yahweh's deliverance. In the Communion feast, the bread and wine become the means of God's grace. If we made our food part of our daily disciplines as faithfully as we make them part of our rituals, we would be healthier. We would have time and money for more significant things and would care more about how the food we eat affects the world.

We are just passing through on a journey that begins with God and ends with God. Along the way, our path is not obstructed by food but is smoother when we stop being driven by it. The Gospels teach us that when we consider the lilies and sparrows, we remember where our treasures lie. The great spiritual leaders didn't worry about food unless it was for someone else. We should strive for the same thing. Food becomes a concern only when we remember those who don't have enough to eat.

LEARNING THE LANGUAGE

I ONCE LEARNED THAT THERE ARE FIVE KINDS OF PRAYER: thanksgiving, petition, lament, praise, and exultation. I think there are probably more than a thousand. Prayers exist for everything we do and see and are; all are legitimate. Prayer is one of the most intimate experiences we have, and so there can't be a single language that works for all people. The conversations that work best are the ones developed over time in relationship. It is a language cultivated in the deep recesses of our hearts, and it works best when practiced alone. It is as private as the way we kiss someone we love. We learn it by listening, repeating, and trying out how it sounds and feels. The deepest prayers are born in a sacred space between head and heart and move from silence into substance.

When I started reflecting on this section, I heard a baby barred owl in the yard, calling out to its mom. Its cry was beautifully symbolic of what the language of prayer feels like to me. When we call out in our prayer for comfort, God must think we sound like baby birds. The owl would not have been singing if it had sensed danger or if it had had a doubt about its mother's care. It reminded me that there is a private prayer language and one reserved for public occasions. This was the private prayer reserved for the intimate relationship between a mother and baby. It was a comforting and beautiful prayer.

The next week, I went on a walk in the woods with a wise Pentecostal friend. He comes amazingly close to praying without ceasing and is free in his use of language. He has been teaching me slowly over the years how to speak in tongues as a chant and how to open my heart to prayer. The practice is foreign to me, but I am awed by the idea and believe I know a little of what he is saying. While he was talking about his prayer language, we encountered a large rattlesnake on the side of the trail. It stopped us dead in our tracks. I made a small joke about how he could "handle" it, but mostly I was frozen in fear and awe. It occurred to me that the rattlesnake, like my friend's prayer language, was wild and unnerving. It was mesmerizing and unpredictable. It was rhythmic and startling. It cut its own way and made others step aside. It was true to its nature and unwavering in its purpose. I respected, feared, and loved it. It brought me close to the heart of God.

When you travel in some parts of the Middle East, a call to prayer comes from tall minarets five times a day. The *muezzin* shouts through huge speakers, *"Allah akbar!"* ("God is great!") The cry echoes through city streets, in the country, along the river bank. Having the whole community called in this fashion is a wonderful way to practice the language of prayer.

Hand motions, body positions, and sacred objects are also helpful. Christian and Muslim traditions include prayer beads. In the Buddhist practice there are mantras and sitting styles. In the Native American tradition there are wonderful drums, and Hinduism has incense and powerful images. I love learning all the new prayer languages, but for most of us our first language will feel the most comfortable. When we learn another language, we always have a slight accent.

In order for us to be in relationship, we have to communicate. So if we want to be in relationship with God, we have to pray. We pray to travel. We pray to live. I have gone through long periods when I feel as though I am talking to the wind. Sometimes I feel the wind and God's presence all in the same breath. The mystery of the language is what draws us in and keeps us close to God.

The styles in which we communicate may vary, but the language is love grounded in a desire to be with God. We have to do whatever it takes for us to pray. We may lock ourselves away, sit in a bathtub, use icons or books, light a candle, close our eyes, breathe deeply, recite old prayers, pray alone or with a community. How we do it is not important. What is important is that we pray every single day of our lives.

Just as important as the prayer itself is our knowledge that others have prayed for us. What we do and how we live have been affected by other people's prayers. After all, the nature of prayer is not that it changes God; it changes us. About three years ago a woman moved into a new Magdalene house. Our community had worked hard to raise the money for its construction. The woman said, "I prayed for a home like this while I was in jail, and now God has answered my prayer." At first I was skeptical; but when I really thought about it, the idea made sense. The work we had all been doing may have been motivated in part by prayers we had never known. The language of prayer is deep and silent and moves the world in ways we cannot fathom.

I had thought my job was to pray for others. Through that woman I learned that prayer may also be involved when I am open to service and loving my neighbor. Prayer is the web connecting us to one another and to God. It is the basis of our relationship with the Holy One and the means by which we live in the Spirit.

Prayer can lead to healing, but I have never used it as magic. When I visit someone who is sick, I lay hands on them. Part of my prayer is that God will heal them in body, mind, and spirit so that they will never forget the healing power of God's love. I have oils blessed by a community and psalms to read. All these are beautiful expressions of prayer. And the truth is, I want those for myself. When I am sick or near death, I want someone to offer a prayer of hope and love, someone who will use the best language when I have lost my own. What I don't want is for someone to think that because I died, the prayer was not faithful or beautiful.

BREAD FOR THE JOURNEY

BREAD IS A STAPLE FOR PILGRIMS IN MANY TRADITIONS. IT IS a simple, filling food, easy to share with those who are hungry.

Pita, sometimes called "Arabic bread," is a round, leavened Middle Eastern flat bread. It is used to scoop sauces and dips such as hummus and to wrap meats. It usually can be found at *iftar*, the evening meal in the month of Ramadan, the time when Muslims fast during the day in order to concentrate on worship and contemplation.

Matzah is flat, crispy, cracker-like bread representing the hastily baked bread of the Israelites on their flight from Egypt. It has a central place at the Seder, a ritual on the first night of Passover. In keeping with tradition, it is not allowed to rise; and in kosher cooking no more than eighteen minutes may elapse from the time the water is mixed with flour until the matzah is put into the oven.

Chapattis is the unleavened, round bread of India. It is cooked on the stovetop and is used to scoop food, usually vegetables, as the Hindu tradition favors a vegetarian way of life to recognize living things.

Bread in the Christian tradition, served at the altar in the Eucharist, represents the body of Christ. It is traditionally unleavened because the Last Supper, when Jesus broke bread and gave it to his disciples, was the Jewish Passover meal. The invitation is universal: Take this bread and eat it. Remember where you came from and where you are headed. Remember that what you eat is an important expression of who you are and how you want to live.

Bread offers a symbolic, tangible sign of God's loving presence in our daily lives.

helpful hints

- Proclaim original grace wherever you go. Each one of us is made in the image of God. As we walk into the world and into our hearts, it is helpful to see each person on the road as a fellow traveler whose journey began not with original sin but original grace. All our stories begin and end with God, so this is a journey back to wholeness.

- You may never be able to pray without ceasing; but whenever you realize that you are not praying, think of God.

- Think of prayer as working out, and practice praying. Practice fasting, using prayer beads, sitting in silence, writing in a journal, and reading holy writings. Then repeat a thousand times those acts that help you pray.

- Whenever you encounter another traveler, just say, "There goes God" instead of "There but for the grace of God go I." Every person should be treated with love and respect.

- It is better to take the longer path. There is no short-cut on this journey; and it is definitely a walk, not a run. Think of it as exercising your heart muscles. If given a choice between a quick walk to the car or a long stroll through the woods, take the stroll and use the time to pray and listen for God's voice in the woods.

A Prayer for This Moment

Thank you, God, for this moment
For all the moments leading to this moment
For all the people who were part of all those moments
For all the people we love who have died
For all the people we love who are walking with us
For every kind deed done and left undone to us
For every ounce of forgiveness we have ever known
For all those whose hearts we have broken to get here
For all those who broke our hearts to get us here
For everything that we remember
*   and everything we have forgotten*
Thank you.

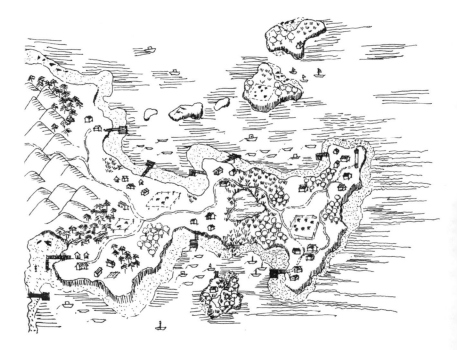

3. traveling well

A Resurrection Witness

Of course I saw a bluebird on the way home
And a thunderstorm passed by
*   and beat on my chest*
And a hawk cut through a slate gray sky
And the song was sung by angels
And the sky parted and cleared
And every flower and bush burst into blossom
And Jesus broke my heart wide open
And the stone was rolled away.

WALKING WELL-WORN PATHS

When I was in New Orleans a few years ago, I walked around the French Quarter early in the morning. The only people I saw were vendors, artists, and a fortuneteller who were setting up their stalls before the people began to arrive. The fortuneteller wore 1970s medieval clothing with long earrings, and gravity pulled hard on her shoulders. I was in line to get coffee when I heard one of the vendors ask the fortuneteller, "What happened yesterday?" She said, "I went to the hospital because I thought I was having a heart attack. I was wrong, though. I'm fine. It was just some anxiety." Perfect, I thought. A fortuneteller who can't read her own future.

It's like that sometimes. Others can't really help us find our way, because they have never been there either. That's not to say, however, that the experience of others can't be helpful. It is almost impossible to forge a new path, a path completely our own in virgin woods. It is better to root ourselves in a tradition and learn from pilgrims who have walked there before. For example, we can learn much about faith from the eight-fold path given to the Buddha in the shade of the bodhi tree. We have commandments handed down to Moses on Mount

Sinai to guide us. Teachings given to Mohammed (blessings be upon him) by Allah in the desert lead millions to make pilgrimages to Mecca. Teachings in Hinduism have changed the way we treat animals and seek peace. These traditions are so basic that it seems almost ridiculous to repeat them here, but it is surprising how many intelligent people discard whole faiths before ever cracking the spine of a text.

Those same people wouldn't dream of discarding past learnings in mathematics. They learn to find the length of a hypotenuse of a triangle by adding the squares of the sides and taking the square root of that sum. It isn't until much later that they begin to prove the theorems and then the axioms that make up those theorems; but in our lives of faith, we start to dismantle the theorems of faith before spending time applying the principles and practicing.

I have heard people say, "I'm spiritual, not religious." That statement has always rung in my ears as a little arrogant. If religion is the practice of spiritual principles, then being "spiritual" but not having a religion is just holding a set of ideas that you never practice. Religion is a discipline, and all of us need some discipline. I know faithful people who, having practiced a religion for years, have moved beyond its borders to grow and expand their universe. In fact, a great theologian in the twentieth century said it was inevitable that pilgrims move beyond their boundaries to realize a universal God. The point is that we might want to claim that we are religious (practice a discipline) before announcing we are spiritual (hold spiritual beliefs). According to St. Augustine, being spiritual means that we have the ability to reflect on our lives and thoughts. Our reflection is influenced by what we do and say and pray. So it is good to begin our walk by doing, reading, and reflecting on the best sources, knowing that we will become more spiritual as we progress.

In the Catholic tradition, the church teaches that we don't always believe what we pray. Instead, we pray what we hope to believe. We keep doing the right thing, showing gratitude through our actions, surrendering to our faith, and trusting the rest will come our way. No one can walk for us; we have to do it ourselves. We won't believe just because other people believe, and we won't be religious if we never do the work.

Several years ago a woman walked into my office after her husband died. She wanted me to organize a memorial service; and when we sat down to write out the liturgy, she pulled out prayers and themes from several different traditions that didn't seem to go together. As near as I could tell, her husband was going to meet his mother on the other side of Jordon, be reincarnated, and travel to Nirvana. Now, I am open to all faiths and was thankful to help a grieving widow; but I just couldn't figure out what we were doing. I kept thinking how hard it must have been for her to wander for years, holding all kinds of ideas without much cohesion. When she needed to fall back on faith, it was almost impossible. It broke my heart to watch her sit in my office asking, "What should I do now?" I saw her that day as a beautiful dancer who had never actually bothered to try out any moves. Most of her dancing consisted of watching other people, critiquing how they danced, and deciding that she wouldn't want to dance as they did. Finally, when she was called forward to dance, her steps looked awkward and were hard to watch.

I do believe that we are born with everything we need for the journey; but the gifts we receive from birth need to be cultivated, honed, and trained. We need to write moral laws on our hearts and memorize sacred texts that can be mantras. We need to practice the tenets of faith to the best of our ability so that when called upon we can dance.

LISTENING TO THE BIRDS

ONE MORNING JUST ABOUT SUNRISE, THERE WAS A BEAUTIFUL concert of birds—not a note out of tune. They were singing all at the same time and yet individually and in beautiful harmony. As I heard the songs, I started thinking about the parade of birds that have flown in and out of my life.

The birds come out faithfully every morning, intone us to an awakened state, and later sing the sun to bed. Even if we never learn their names or songs, the birds can connect us to God's voice and creation. I can hear them when I walk in the woods and listen at my window. In the densest city, the hardy pigeons and starlings still sing and hold out hope for nature's will to live.

I have never studied the birds except by observation and kind friends who have helped me to see and hear them. My hope is to be a worthy disciple, to watch and listen to their signs. I want to learn through them to trust that life is unfolding as it should and that I need to walk the path that is before me. I love hearing stories of other travelers who talk about seeing birds as signs. One person told me he saw a sparrow chase a hawk and thought of his father; another saw a robin in spring and found mercy in the sight.

I like to remember all that the birds have taught me. When I see a cardinal and hear the clear click of its song, I sense that something good is coming. When the mockingbird sets up near me, I know that I have been taking life too seriously. When the hawk cuts through the gray sky, the Spirit of God is close. When swallows fly, I have work to do. When the crow comes through, I need to listen more closely. When the heron calls me back to myself, I remember that all I need is found in creation. When the buzzards come together, I remember the gift of community. When the sparrow gets caught in my house, I remember to cherish all the people I love.

For years my husband has played a game with our three boys. They lie down in the yard on their backs with their arms tucked behind their heads and look up into the sky. The game is simply to count the birds and call out the number. Sometimes they get lost in cloud shapes; but more often then not they just lie still, looking up at an eternal sky to celebrate every bird that crosses their path. Flocks of white doves cause an explosion of shouts. Robins, pigeons, and starlings are as worthy and welcome as a bluebird.

On the road to hither and yon, birds have traveled with me the whole way, never asking anything of me other than to listen. Their lessons live between my head and heart, and I carry those lessons on the altar of what I hold dearest in my life.

WALKING IN THE WOODS

THERE IS NOTHING BETTER FOR THE SPIRIT THAN TO WALK IN the woods. It is in the silence of nature—listening for the birds, animals, and wind—that we hear God speak. Many people believe that living out a life of faith apart from a relationship with nature is impossible. That is simply to say, go to the woods.

Go there in every season so that you can see the trees transformed in the course of a year. Go to see the first spring flowers awaken from their sleep, when these brave and tender early risers in unison call creation back to life. Go in the heat of the summer, when the air is heavy and big and hearty plants stand hunched faithfully in the heat of the day. Go on cloudy days in the early morning, at sunset, or whenever you are feeling the need to see more clearly. Whenever you go, you can trust nature to open your mind and heart and to quiet your fears. It is in the woods where I have learned that mountains can be made to look like molehills if I get enough distance on them.

One year when I was feeling completely overwhelmed by the work of living, I took to the woods. My feeling was that if I never heard another preacher, it would be a gift. If I never had to raise another dime for a program I was running, it would be a great blessing. I was exhausted, and I didn't even know it. I couldn't have found my way down a spiritual path if there had been huge signs with my name in bold letters and arrows pointing out the path; but in walking and praying, I caught the wonderful smell of wisteria. It reminded me that even when I doubt God's Spirit, when I am unable to trust my own thoughts about God or other preachers, somehow I believe in the wildflowers.

I am not a gardener; I am just a worshiper of the gardens in creation. I believe in the softness of the lavender in thistles that is tucked behind the thorns and in the yellow of the buttercups strewn extravagantly across fields. I believe in the white of the Queen Anne's Lace that is more intricate than the best tatting and in the brown of the Black-eyed Susans multiplying a hundredfold in the sun. I believe in the sweetness of the roadside honeysuckle. I believe in the smell of peonies overflowing with the joy of spring, in the freshness of the morning glory that greets each dawn, in the grandeur of the sunflower that will find its place in the sun. I believe in the humility of the bluets whose crosses lie next to the black earth and the green grass, in the faithfulness of the iris that grow every spring, in the tenderness of the wild orchids that wither in a harsh world, in the dignity of the columbine that reach through cracks in rocks and bow their heads in thankfulness. I believe these flowers were created by the magnificent Gardener who knows they speak to us.

We have believed in flowers a long time; and that is why we offer them on important occasions, including birth, marriage, and death. We lay them on our altars, we spray our bodies with their fragrances, and we name our loveliest daughters after them. I believe that their colors and fragrances speak to our hearts about God's Spirit. So whenever we wonder about the institutional religions of the world or how to find God, we are invited to breathe the scent of the flowers and have a revival out in the woods. Every time we find a new flower or come across an old familiar one, we can genuflect and give thanks to God for such a beautiful gift, offered to us as freely as grace on our path.

TRAVELING ON THE FRINGES

IF WE THINK OF LIFE AS A SERIES OF SIDE TRIPS ON A WOVEN cloth made up of all the roads, then the spiritual path is located on the fringes of that cloth. There is something about the fringes of life that affords us a view of the beautiful fabric of the world, allowing us to watch the unfolding of the pattern and critique its design. The fringes are the vantage point of poets and artists. They are places of margin and loosely collected ends that don't hold together. Much like the spiritual journey itself, working and living on the fringes can make us feel free and lonely. The fringes are woven on one end and flying freely on the other. Walking there can take you easily to the woods, to the hospitals, and to the homes of people who are suffering and moving along the fringes themselves.

My friend's mother is dying of a cancer that has taken over her mind and body. In the process, her world has continued to shrink so that it fits into a small condo with about eight or nine people who watch after her. She talks some, but many of her words are confused; and she can no longer recognize common household items, such as coffee cans or pencils. Going to see her is a journey into the fringes of life. You must make the effort—you are not going to run into her at the store. Stepping inside this separate and tiny world of hers is a powerful and dramatic experience. In some ways it feels surreal and completely humbling, contemplating how life can bring us back to our infancy in death.

During one visit, as I watched the woman's son take her hand and escort her into the kitchen, I unexpectedly encountered another dreamier world sitting on the second shelf of a curio cabinet. Evidently, years ago when raising five children and retreating to novels in her bedroom, she had collected ceramic palaces that looked like magical kingdoms—a German palace from the mountains, a Russian palace straight out of the movie *Dr. Zhivago*, a Moroccan palace from the turn of the century with a dozen golden domes surrounding a courtyard. I saw the palaces as daydreams that spoke to her longings and wishes. I saw them as secrets telling the viewer that this woman had private thoughts that no one would know about her, even in her death. I saw them as evidence of the fringes in all our lives and of how they can make a life richer and deeper.

Somehow we have to find our way to the fringes so that we don't get caught up in trying to keep all that we have in place. Most of the great prophets and activists were never accepted into the mainstream. They danced on the edges, able to speak freely and travel lightly. On the fringes we can daydream easily, have time to take in a clear sky, and spend time with other people on the margins who could use our help. From that vantage point we can see everything in our lives weaving together to become part of a great tapestry.

When I was young, I worked in Coventry Cathedral in England. There were so many beautiful things about the cathedral, but the tapestry in the front was probably the most stunning. Considered the largest tapestry in the world, it depicts Jesus as the bridegroom welcoming the church, his bride, to his throne. I was astonished to learn that it took two generations of weavers to complete the tapestry. The people who started the weaving never saw the end of their work. Trusting that the image of God would emerge through the whole, they just kept weaving their corner of the fabric, moving on the fringes.

TAKING RIGHT ACTION

THE SPIRITUAL PATH COMES DOWN TO LOVING GOD, NEIGHBORS, and self. The rest will work itself out. Whenever we feel lost and wonder if God is real or why the innocent suffer, we can ask ourselves some questions that will set us right in a hurry. Did I feed anyone who was hungry today? Did I tell anyone that I loved them? Did I work toward peace and justice? Did I offer thanks for my breath?

The lyrics of the old Shaker hymn say it well.

> 'Tis the gift to be simple,
> 'tis the gift to be free,
> 'Tis the gift to come down
> where we ought to be,
> And when we find ourselves
> in the place just right,
> 'Twill be in the valley
> of love and delight.

Right actions on the journey are the way to get to the place of love and delight. I heard someone say that a faith separated from the economics of the world doesn't hold water. I think that person was right. If we are not concerned about war, poverty, and justice, we are praying hollow words. If what we contemplate in our hearts doesn't well up in us and cause us to act, then we need to contemplate again.

I have been thinking about the issues surrounding gay and lesbian rights to ordination and same-sex blessings within faith communities. Truly, in the last hundred years it has been the most divisive issue in church politics, next to women's ordination and segregation. People are more passionate about it than about starving children. I have known how I felt about this issue for years. To me, it has always seemed more like a pastoral issue than a doctrinal issue. During the early years of my ministry, I chose not to become actively involved in the struggle for gay rights, because I didn't want to be the pastor of a gay church or a straight church. I wanted simply to be a priest in a church where people's sexuality and spirituality could be integrated. Whenever a single issue defines a church, we end up picking sides; and I didn't want necessarily to be on any team. I think to organize a church around sexual orientation is deplorable. What I would rather have is an open and welcoming church that doesn't define people by their orientation and can move on to caring for the most vulnerable in the community.

In 2003, however, when a vote came up at the General Convention of the Episcopal Church in Minneapolis, there was no way to avoid the issue. The convention had to decide whether or not to ratify the election to bishop in New Hampshire of an openly gay priest named Gene Robinson. No matter what was decided, it was going to be costly for the church. I knew that, for me, right action in this situation meant defending the rights of people who were gay or lesbian. Faith communities were attacking people and questioning their faith solely based on their sexual orientation. As a result, I became one of seven people chosen to speak on the floor of the convention on Gene Robinson's behalf.

I said that I remembered my father, who was an Episcopal priest, say he believed that it would be the end of the church if women were ordained. He died in 1968, before the first woman was ordained. In 1991, I was ordained two weeks before the birth of my first son. Six years later, twenty-nine years after my father's death, my husband and I asked our son what he wanted to be when he grew up. When we suggested he could be a priest, he made a funny face and said, "A priest! That's a girl's job." I told the convention that I had only dreamed of my father once since he died; but that the night before, I had dreamed about him. I saw him lift his hand to help me stand at the mike and tell everyone not to worry. Let Gene be a bishop; and then get on with the work of the church, which is to clothe the naked and feed the hungry and love our enemies. If we do that work, the church will survive.

When I came home, I was amazed by the anger of people in my diocese. They were furious with me. One woman wrote that I should never again call myself Christian. A man who had served as a priest with my father said that I had desecrated the memory and ministry of my father. On top of everything else, I was stricken with Bell's Palsy, a temporary facial paralysis, for about three weeks. Eighteen months later, Gene Robinson wrote me a kind letter in which he said he remembered the speech as one of the most powerful moments of the convention and hoped I had not paid too high a price for what I had done. I kept thinking how small a price I had paid, compared with those who had been on the receiving end of hatred for their sexual orientation. I paid about a penny to hold my views, and I am grateful for the experience.

Maybe it is a requirement to have faith cost you something. The other requirement is to love people standing on the other side of the line. What I don't ever want is to be separated from others just because we feel differently on a particular issue. I know faithful people who feel differently about issues even closer to home, such as women's ordination. Standing together in prayer and communion is sometimes the only way we can communicate and understand God's mercy for us. Loving those on the other side of an issue doesn't mean that we stop speaking the truth in love or performing acts of justice. Those actions help set us on the right path. I believe faith will follow from that.

If you look at the lives of great pilgrims, most of them had conversion experiences that led them to take radical positions about justice in the world. In many cases, those experiences were the only way the pilgrims would have had the courage and strength to confront powers and principalities in the name of justice or on behalf of those with no power. This is true for us, too. We have to feel the conversion toward right action. This is the place on the journey where I hear my mother's voice call out, "You had better snap out of it." It's time to quit worrying about how it will affect us if we act in accordance with what we believe. It's time to think about how we can live faithfully if we do not act.

helpful hints

- Remember that even though you are traveling alone, you can carry communities with you. While the journey is lonely, you can share the experiences, joys, and sorrows with those in your community.

- Pray for humor to carry you on the journey. It is a great gift to be able to laugh at yourself.

- Don't worry that what you do in the name of justice might not make a difference. Walk with conviction that if you offer your life and heart to the journey, you will never be the same.

- Don't forget your roots. There is a place—for better or for worse—that you call home. It is where you learned how to walk and talk. Remember its lessons as you move beyond them.

- Celebrate the knowledge that small changes make all the difference. Sometimes the miracle of healing and love happens so slowly that we forget to notice the great difference that has occurred in our lives.

- It's hard to love the sinner and hate the sin. In my experience the fascination with the details of the sin and its consequences far outweigh the love offered the sinner. On this road try first to love the sinner. When you have figured that out, then you can move toward hating the sin.

A Prayer for Guidance

Holy God, the giver and sustainer of all life,
Keep me close when I can't find my way.
Surround me with your presence,
Anoint my head with the balm of peace,
Show me your work in the world around me.
Teach me again what it means to fall in love,
  not using my lips
But in the deepest part of my heart
  and with my whole being.
Amen.

4. persevering

Dark Nights

Where are the birds?
The predators are out,
But they are keeping a low profile.
I can't read the stars,
So I'm without a map
And just feel the night
Calling me to sit awhile.

This is the darkest night I have known.
I am melting into it
And being carried to oblivion.
If I am allowed one prayer,
Even if I don't believe a word of it,
I pray that the dawn is coming
And the birds will remember to sing.

KEEP WALKING UNTIL
THE BAD SPIRITS GET BORED

MY FIRST MISSION TRIP AS A CANDIDATE FOR ORDINATION WAS to the Rosebud Reservation, a Sioux settlement in South Dakota. I organized a group of teens from Franklin, Tennessee, to study Native American spirituality based on a curriculum from the National Episcopal and United Methodist churches. We raised enough money to make a week-long trip that was to include classes with some of the reservation teachers and a two-day pow-wow experience.

All of us were excited as we drove for hours from Tennessee to a small village in South Dakota. We went through orientation and prepared to attend the pow-wow on the third day. That morning we dressed and set out early to find seats. Over the next several hours, people entered and slowly made the place ready for a gathering. Finally the dancers came and the drumming began. As we watched, dancers began to move in small, slow, rhythmic steps. The drumming got louder, but it never got faster. For several hours, while the slow dance kept going around the circle, people would get up to talk and eat. When I realized this was it and I wasn't going to miss a big finale if I got up to move around, I also decided to eat.

When I returned to my seat, I relaxed and began to think of the movements as more of a trance than a dance. The dancers continued into the night and picked up the next day where they had stopped. Some of our group, feeling they had already experienced the pow-wow, sat by the campsite most of the day; but the rest of us made our way back and watched people move in a circle to the drums for the next two days. Years later, I read that part of the reason for the dance was to bore the bad spirits so they would cross over the mountains and leave. As I read those words, I saw the pow-wow in my mind and thought about how we had wanted to leave. I could picture the drums so clearly that I started to hear them in my prayer. I imagined that the drummers had been playing the whole time and that I was just beginning to tune them in again.

The journey to hither and yon is not always exciting. It is more like a slow dance. In fact, I am feeling as if I am at the beginning of the dance and all the bad spirits are just starting to get bored. It has taken thousands of prayers. It has taken loaves of small bites of Communion. It has taken gallons of sips of wine. I am slowly learning the steps and hearing the drums. The dance is one of steady, rhythmic movements to the beat of a constant drum, without a big finale or a crowd-pleasing flip. The promise is that we will find the strength to keep moving until the dance is over.

In the thirteenth century, a mystic and poet named Rumi was asked to describe the mystic Sufi Attar. Rumi said that Attar, whose religion was known for its dance, spent thirty-nine years reaching the perfection of an eagle by creeping like an ant.

In our walk, we are called to dance the old dance together and to persevere. We are called to dance until we bore the politics out of church. To dance until we forget resentments and the need to control. To dance until fear subsides and war is over and impotency is forgotten. To dance until pride loses track and sickness scars over. To dance until the prison walls fall into a river of reconciliation and wholeness. To dance until all that remains is the desire to preach love and to surrender. To dance until the ground feels nothing but fertile and acceptance and truth become a way of life. To dance slowly and steadily until the drums are part of our hearts and we know what praying ceaselessly means. To dance until all that remains is love.

THE JOURNEY ISN'T FAIR

ONE OF THE SUREST TRUTHS ABOUT THIS JOURNEY IS THAT IT is not fair. It is as unfair as a woman trying to get pregnant for fifteen years while a fifteen-year-old gets pregnant by mistake. It is as unfair as a child getting cancer or war taking a civilian's life. It is as unfair as being judged by the color of your skin or the scarf on your head.

At one time or another, all of us have said, "It's not fair." I know it has crossed my mind when people get something I think they do not deserve. It can be caused by something as ridiculous as getting passed over in line or not having my child picked to take a turn. When I become distracted on the journey by just how unfair it is, I remember a mantra I heard as a child, delivered by my widowed mother raising five children: "Who promised you fair?" If my mother was in a bad mood, she might add, "You might as well get the suitcase from the hall closet and move if you are looking for fair."

Now, in my role as director of Magdalene, I find myself repeating that mantra. One woman will get an overnight pass; another will receive her stipend sooner; and someone fairly new to the program will call me and complain, "It's not fair!" Sounding more like my mother than I ever dreamed possible, I snap back, "Who promised you fair? We said we would do the best we can for you, and that is all." If I am in a bad mood, I will add, "You might as well get your suitcase and move, because it's never going to be fair."

This is not a bad phrase to carry with us on the road, although it's not a tender expression. It helps us to accept all the manifestations of God's love that we encounter. Everyone, having been made in the image of God, is the beloved child of God—the prostitute, the tax collector, the priest, the good neighbor. Everyone is no more and no less than every other child of God. The part that feels unfair to some is that there is no economy of salvation, where points are earned and rewards given. But think about it: How well would any of us do if God's grace were in proportion to our works and beliefs? When we complain that the world is not fair, what we really need to ask ourselves is this: "Why would we begrudge God's generosity toward anybody else in the world, and why would others begrudge God's forgiving us?" Thank God that the world isn't fair!

In the winter of 2005, one of the women in Magdalene went to court on one of the most serious charges we have ever faced as a community. She grew up in a culture where she had to fend for herself, where no one had taught her to read, and where she had been molested. She was a prostitute and addict before her sixteenth birthday. One evening in a haze outside a crack house, a horrible scene unfolded. In the midst of a fight, a man was shot and she was charged. After living in the Magdalene community for almost a year, the woman was convicted of second-degree murder. She had landed in a new world, and now that world was going to sort out justice. She had been part of a system of betrayal and abuse where guilt and innocence were so obscure that they seemed to make no sense. At her sentencing, she was surrounded by a community of women who had lived with her and helped fight her case. The judge ruled that she would serve no time. He sentenced her to eight years of probation and allowed her to continue to live another year in Magdalene, in a home that is striving to show that love is the most powerful force for change in this world. It was overwhelming to watch in that moment as the scales of justice broke, and all that was left was a woman standing before God in gratitude.

Sometimes the journey to hither and yon seems like one step forward and two steps back. It is moving toward love with courage and then being willing to surrender. It is moving toward silence and then abandoning it to speak out. It is moving toward believing we can fly and then letting ourselves fall. It is relying on faith while knowing that faith alone is not enough. Our only hope, finally, is that we will forget where we are in line long enough to help our brothers and sisters get ahead.

WALK FARTHER
THAN YOU MEANT

THERE IS A STORY IN THE GOSPELS ABOUT THE DISCIPLES getting into their boat. The story says that Jesus ordered them to go. I believe that Jesus called them into the boat and they felt compelled to do as he asked. The boat took the disciples out farther than they had intended to go. When a storm blew in, the disciples were afraid. Finally, Jesus came to them in their crisis; and they found their faith strengthened by the struggle.

This story is a wonderful illustration of the journey we are on. The disciples hesitated even to get into the boat; then it carried them past the point of safety. They never imagined how far the boat would take them, on the water that day or in the days of their ministry.

We journey to hither and yon because God has called us. Something within us compels us to answer. So we get into the boat, and we go farther than we had ever intended. We see great sights. We have the wind at our backs. We are pushed by the winds of the world beyond our comfort zone and we hear God's voice. We have dark nights, fears, and visions of death; and if we can risk it all and go out deeper still, we will be able to say, "Oh, my God, I almost didn't go. I was almost too afraid; but I followed my heart, thank God."

As I write these words, I am surrounded by about two hundred fifty men and women in desert camouflage being sent to Iraq. Some probably just signed up for the reserves. Others may have wanted to change their minds after joining. Still others may have mixed feelings about their mission; but now they are in the boat, and I imagine there will be nights of wrestling with fear and demons in the desert. My prayer is that they will find a place where the sea is calm and they can find the strength to keep going.

Finally, as Julian of Norwich wrote, "All will be well, and all shall be well, and all will be well." No matter what or where or who we are in our lives, what illness we suffer, or what challenges we face, all will be well. We just have to keep going out farther. The call is to keep sailing, not to safer waters but to the places where we are called to travel, which means going in at least up past our necks. If we don't go in that deep, we will never know the gift of having faith hold us up. Then, whenever we take a step forward, even though it seems perfectly logical that we will sink, we can feel ourselves begin to float.

WHEN BAD THINGS HAPPEN ON THE WAY

THINGS HAPPEN ON THE WAY. THAT IS WHY IT TOOK JESUS three years to travel from Nazareth to Jerusalem, a distance of about two hundred miles. That is why the Buddha had to travel his whole adult life. The stories of hither and yon are stories of "on the way." They often begin something like this: "On the way to the grocery, I saw an old friend." Most of the time these are beautiful stories that help ground us in the world or make us remember what we still need to work on. Many times the stories renew our spirit and give us insight into our hearts. But every now and then, horrific things happen that change the course of our paths forever.

I have listened to stories most of my life. In all the stories I have heard in my role as priest and director of Magdalene, the stories of victims are the hardest to bear. They are so painful and full of sadness that it's tempting to try to take the victim's pain away, but I have too much respect for the story and the person ever to try doing that. The stories about violent and tragic events are rooted in a time and place. They are specific and unique in the world. Therefore, I imagine the ground on which they took place to be sacred ground. It is sacred because from that place, we can contemplate the whole universe. It is sacred because from that experience, the rest of our lives begin. It is sacred because that is where we learn that what we thought would cut us down can form the roots of our faith in God, and it is sacred because God walks that ground with us.

My first memory of standing on that kind of sacred ground happened when I was about six. I was in an old white house. The house was being used as a fellowship hall for the church. We were having a spaghetti supper, and most of the kids were getting their plates and going upstairs to eat. One of the leaders of the church called me into a side room where he molested me for the first time. My memory of it is vague, except I remember that I never dropped the plate I was holding. It was the beginning of a couple of years of sporadic terror. That ground became sacred, because it was where my heart for women on the streets was born and where I took my first steps on the long and difficult path toward healing and forgiveness that was thirty years in the making.

Ultimately we must walk that path alone. Our journey, like our death, is between us and God; but there are ways in which others can share the pain and honor the path. If the places where we are wounded are sacred ground, it would be wonderful for the whole community to treat it as such. When someone begins to tell their story, we could have a ritual of taking off our shoes as Moses did when he stood in front of the burning bush. We could offer incense in recognition that God is close. We could listen to the story without breaking our silence until we heard the whole truth. Then, even though we might not be able to imagine what the experience was like, we could bow our heads and extend a hand. The best way to honor one another's stories is to remember that we are walking in unity as we make our paths alone. I can't walk that ground for you, and you can't walk it for me; but we can share one another's stories by listening, being a friend or counselor, not trying to make it go away, and not forgetting it.

If the story is honored and respected by the whole community, then the victim can begin to see the event as a precious pearl born in pain. As the story is heard by others, the shell enclosing this pearl that is the victim's alone in all the world finally opens up. There is a story in the Gospel of a pearl so powerful and expensive, a man sells everything he owns in order to purchase the land where the pearl is hidden. Like that man, we go back again and again to the events that bore our pearls and that have cost us so dearly to claim as our own.

Then, the Gospel reminds us that we don't cast those pearls before swine. We don't waste the sacred ground and the pearl born there by allowing it to be bought and sold by others who don't understand or value it. All the stories of tragic events belong to the victims and are theirs to share when and with whom they choose. We can't fix the victims. We can only marvel at their strength, cry at their openness, mourn for their losses. Ultimately, those stories are between them and God.

CAN'T SEE THE SPIDER
FOR GOD

I WALKED ON A TRAIL IN NOVEMBER. THE FALL HAD BEEN LATE in coming, and I had almost stopped looking for the trees to change. October had been dry, and so it made sense that the fall had been less than spectacular. As I walked, something sparkled on the periphery of my vision; and I turned my head to see what it was. There, suspended among the leaves, was a spider web glistening in the sunlight.

The web was a tatted masterpiece. It was beautiful and made me feel alive. I almost couldn't see the leaves for that web; but then they, too, came into focus, and I saw the star-shaped leaves of the gum tree making a gorgeous pattern around the web. I almost couldn't see the trees for the leaves, but then I noticed the golden auras of those trees standing tall and holy. I almost couldn't see the forest for the trees, but then I stepped back a little and took it all in. In that moment the forest became an ode to the last days of fall, and I wanted to hold it like a wilting bouquet.

I almost couldn't see the owl for the forest; but then I spotted him staring at me, awake and perched in the middle of that glorious day. The owl is a sign for wisdom, so I sat and watched him to see if he would offer me an insight; and so I almost couldn't see the sky for the owl, but then I finally lifted my head up and saw all the hues of the rainbow blended into the clear expanse. I almost couldn't see God for the beauty of that sky; but when I finally did, I felt at peace and thought that if I died later that day I would recognize heaven. Then I went back to see the web, but the sun in the heavens had moved so the web had become invisible. I couldn't see the spider for God.

The spiritual journey calls us always to remember the sacredness of the web, even when we get to see God. The web leads us along the path to God, and we are wise not to lose sight of it. I think it is possible for visions of God to get in the way of seeing the beauty before us.

TO HELL AND BACK

So far in this travel guide, I have not spoken of hell. That is not because I am afraid of the topic or worried about judgment. I have seen hell a few times. You can find it on Dickerson Road, a street with motels to rent by the hour and where another pedophile was arrested last week. It is where women walk to exchange sex for drugs and lives are sold to the lowest bidders. People dread driving down this road. Some women who have left it behind return to spread the word to other women that you don't have to stay in hell forever. But even on Dickerson Road I believe there is God.

Going to hell is a legitimate part of the spiritual journey. When I first started listening to the stories of women from the streets, nearly all of them said, "It was hell." Women described gang rapes in motels where, upon exiting, the men threw crack on the bed so the women wouldn't have to walk to get stoned again. As I tried to focus on the story of one woman, I had difficulty looking at her face because she couldn't use her left eye. A "john" had stabbed her with a screwdriver. After a couple of years of listening to the stories, I realized I was hearing war stories; and war is hell. So in large part, my job at Magdalene has become one of listening to stories of hell. It was then that I vowed never to be presumptuous and think that I was introducing a woman from the streets to a spiritual journey. If you have been to hell, you are already on a powerful spiritual journey. If you have been to hell, you probably know more about mercy than most of us. I have learned that people who have been to hell and back never again need to worry about judgment hanging over their heads. They need to hear about love a thousand times, so they can experience healing.

I have seen the hell of people's lives and witnessed scenes that I thought I couldn't bear. I can remember seeing a young mother the day after her mastectomy and a beautiful twenty-one-year-old man sentenced to prison for two years. Once in Guatemala, I watched a family sorting through a field of trash in a dump site for their food and clothing. I think I have even graced the gates of hell myself, or as close as I know them to be. So I believe this is a journey we need to take without judgment hanging over our heads. It is a journey to take believing that our life is a gift. We journey through hither and yon not out of fear or obligation but out of deep gratitude. Even though we have tasted hell, love can live in us and through us and after us.

Nine years ago, I met a woman who had been on the streets for a decade. She moved into one of the Magdalene residences; and one afternoon when I happened to stop by, she was mowing the lawn. I told her that she had done a good job and thanked her for her effort. Then she began to question me about whether I noticed she had trimmed it and mowed in straight lines. When I said yes, she asked me if I really liked the way she mowed and if I thought she had done a good job. About three or four times I praised her before I realized that part of the cost of her hell was that it robbed her completely of self-esteem. So for two years she mowed the grass, and I told her how wonderful it all was. When she graduated from the program, she started her own cleaning and mowing business. Praise, not the threat of hell, is good medicine.

I do not worry on this journey about heaven or hell. I have chosen simply to give over this life to love, believing that it will be enough to carry me when I die. Whatever it means to end our lives with God and return to God, it all comes down to love.

helpful hints

- When you are overcome by the big questions, such as "Does God exist?" don't wait for an answer; just keep the faith. Sometimes the big questions can make you feel as though you are paralyzed. Going back to the work of faith allows faith to do the work in us.

- Faith is not a closed system to be argued. It is a story unfolding in our lives.

- On the darkest nights, be willing to accept the darkness rather than giving up the struggle to believe. When you are completely confused and doubt everything, accept the doubt rather than abandoning faith and community.

- Use therapy and servant work to heal your deepest wounds.

- In all history, the most beautiful prayers of praise were raised after tribulation.

- Be willing to abandon old images of God that keep us from growing in the Spirit.

- Sometimes we can take the dreams and signs we see literally.

- The walk toward faith is noble. To abandon it and be a cynic is the easier path, but it doesn't seem to lead anywhere.

A Prayer to Keep Going

I am ready to keep climbing
    even though the mountain is steep.
I am willing to keep searching
    even though the clouds are thick.
I am able to keep praying
    even though the words are flat.
Take these offerings, my Lord, and use them
So that I am surprised by what happens
    when I reach the top and the clouds part.
Amen.

5. stories
for the road

Jesus Hangs Over the Mantle

Jesus hangs like game over the mantle,
Bagged and stuffed.
Forever holding out his arms
That in a passing glance look like horns.
Looking holier than thou,
    neck straining toward the door.
If I had enough nerve
I'd take him down and give him
    a proper burial.

Beneath the mantle, beside the marble altar,
    Jesus stands,
Offering a prayer, neck stooped
    and arms heavy-laden.
If I had enough nerve I'd quit seeking the dead
    among the living.
I wouldn't set my Lord above the altar,
    dead and stiff.

COINCIDENCES

THERE ARE ALL KINDS OF COINCIDENCES THAT OCCUR ON THE way to hither and yon. When I become frightened about what may lie ahead, I think back on all the times when strangers and strange occurrences have come together to give me strength. There are two coincidences that stand out in my memory as profoundly reassuring.

The first came one morning when my mother couldn't walk or speak. At the time, my family didn't realize she had contracted a deadly disease that would take her life just six weeks later. I was in the middle of my own trauma that morning, fearing that I had experienced a miscarriage in the ninth week of my third pregnancy. I felt terrible and scared and wondered if I should go to the doctor or go in the ambulance with my mom to find out what in the world was wrong with her. I called my doctor, a close friend, who said I could come in for a quick checkup and then proceed to the hospital. So I went to the doctor, who after examining me said there was no heartbeat and confirmed the miscarriage.

Afterward I hurried over to the hospital just as a nurse was wheeling my mother into the emergency room. The nurse looked up at me and said, "Anne Stevens? Was she married to a priest named Joe Stevens?" "Yes," I said, "but he died back in 1968." The nurse's question was like a comforting drink of hot tea after a long walk in a cold drizzle. No one in my whole adult life had ever asked me that question. My father had only been in Nashville for eighteen months before he was killed on my mother's birthday by a drunk truck driver. The way I had always heard the story of his death was that he had left a morning service, had stopped by a house to help someone, and then on the way home to eat lunch had been killed. The nurse said, "It was my house where your father stopped before he died. My mother and father were having a really hard time, and he spoke with them in our living room. I was just a child, but the story in our family was that he saved their marriage."

I don't know why it had never occurred to me or my siblings to ask about the house my father had visited; but the fact that thirty years later this stranger, on one of the strangest mornings of my life, was saying my father had saved her parents' marriage was completely overwhelming. There she was, a nurse, looking after my mother and loving her. It was one of the most reassuring experiences I have ever known. I still had had a miscarriage and my mother still died, but I experienced healing and no longer thought that my life was spinning out of control. Mercy and grace were standing in front of me, welcoming me to stay and be at peace.

The second coincidence came when my thirty-eight-year-old sister, who had recovered from bone cancer a year earlier, went to the Republic of Cameroon for the summer. Since she is a wonderful teacher and an expert hand therapist, she signed on to teach occupational therapy to students as part of an exchange program. On Sunday morning during the first week of her trip, I received a phone call right after church. My sister had been in a horrible bus accident in which five people had died. The bus had careened over a bridge and into the river, and my sister was lying in a local hospital in Cameroon waiting to be evacuated to Switzerland. Her arms and hands had been crushed, and she had lost a lot of blood. In addition, the river was dirty and infection was likely. The next morning, just as she was being flown to Geneva for surgery, I boarded a plane for Switzerland. I wouldn't know until I landed if she had survived.

I spent part of my time on the airplane reflecting on the sermon I had delivered just before the phone call. I had preached on the good Samaritan story in the Gospel of Luke. For the first time, I had proposed that we are not the Samaritan or the priest or the Levite but the man in the ditch. On the plane, I recalled what I had been told about my sister's accident. Because of the nature and extent of her injuries, she might have drowned in the river; but miraculously a beer distributor from South Africa had seen the accident, pulled my sister from the river, and taken her to the hospital. The doctor had poured alcohol into her wounds and sewed her up as best as he could. Later, my sister would tell me that the doctor asked if she wanted anything before the stitching began. She asked him to recite the Lord's Prayer. Hearing his beautiful accent as she was falling asleep, the words filled her with hope.

Thinking about the good Samaritan and my sister's unquenchable thirst for life, I knew in my heart that she would live. When I arrived, I was greeted by the president of the hospital, who met our every need for the next nine days. My sister endured six surgeries and lost much of the use of her hands and part of her left palm. Ironically, she whose skill was in healing others' hands could no longer even handle change without having it fall through her fingers. My stay in Geneva was the only time in my life that I had ever spent nine days alone with my sister, and I look back on that time as precious and life-changing. Neither one of us took the other for granted during those days, and we passed them crying and laughing freely. She has been able to continue as an occupational therapist; and several years later when one of my sons put his hand through a glass window, she was able to help him achieve a complete recovery. I watched her with great love and awe as she patiently showed him how to move his little finger even though hers was missing.

I don't know what is coincidence, what is lucky, and what is providential. I do know that if we look back on our paths and connect the dots, there is a pattern to God's mercy and love. I am grateful that some of the dots are so peculiar, reminding me to look back so that I can move forward with courage.

A COPTIC CHURCH
IN OLD CAIRO

"*ALLAH AKBAR, ALLAH AKBAR.*"

I was standing in a Coptic church in Old Cairo. Mary and Joseph had fled to this city when Jesus was a small boy. They had come to Egypt, the priest said, because Cairo was where they could find tolerance and protection. A church was erected over the site in the second century to commemorate the exile of Jesus. On the far wall was an original icon depicting the moment when Nicodemus took the nails out of Jesus' feet to take him down from the cross. The painting was almost 1,800 years old, painted just 200 years after Jesus walked over this ground and painted before the Bible was finalized. The details of the Crucifixion seemed clear in the artist's mind, and I could feel the pain and intimacy of the moment. There were no other visitors in the church, because the pyramids and mummies were a bigger draw. The place was peaceful. As I stood in that quiet sanctuary, I noticed a cobweb was settling in the corner of the painting.

The cobweb is a powerful symbol of how everything beautiful and lovely returns to dust. It represents the fall of things that we call treasure and, though harmless in itself, reminds us that even stone goes back to ash and earth. When I noticed the cobweb, I was humbled by its presence. It made me feel fragile. It made me feel small and transient. It reminded me that whatever I write or preach or do will only live as long as a kind friend keeps them alive. So I said a prayer to Nicodemus for all that has returned to dust that was created in love. I brushed the cobweb away, thinking that in some way I had helped to save the painting, at least for another year or so. That may have been my most significant moment in Egypt. Ideally, we may create one piece worth saving; and we are walking well to preserve the offerings of others on the way. Walking the path that Jesus calls us to walk is not just finding our way. It is helping a friend, a stranger, or an artist find his.

"Allah akbar, Allah akbar."

THE BATHROOM
AT THE VATICAN

MY FAMILY WENT TO ROME TO VISIT THE VATICAN. EVEN though I have been washed in its images for as long as I can remember, I wanted the experience of standing in the midst of it.

It was already hot when we got in line, under the shadow of forty-foot saints and rulers, to pass through the metal detector. Once through, we passed the famous brass doors by Bernini and decided to head up the circular stairway into the cupola. There was another line. During the hour-long wait on the huge, circular staircase, we sipped water and slowly passed by mosaics and famous statues in which the Holy Spirit was represented in the finest stone. We reached the top, looked at the magnificence and power of the cupola from on high, and then wandered onto the catwalk of St. Peter's dome. As we looked down on the grandest church in the entire world, I found it literally breathtaking. Wandering the rooftop, we enjoyed the cooler air and the backs of the heads of the sculptures that looked out from the roof.

I walked to a back corner of the roof, and there I met the woman who cleans the bathroom at the top of St. Peter's. I was the only person there. The woman genuflected to the paper towel holder she was restocking and then handed me a clean towel. Her vestment was a blue jumpsuit. To me, her actions felt similar to foot washing. "Grazie," I said, and made a little bow. Somehow tending the bathrooms there seemed like sacred work, and I wanted to honor her role.

As we descended the stairway, circling around and around, I wondered why the woman's role as a bathroom attendant at the Vatican seemed nobler than cleaning the bathroom at a gas station. In my heart, I do not believe that the ground at the Vatican is more sacred than a prison or a forest. I do not believe that breaking bread and sipping wine there is holier than when I perform that act out in the world. If it is true that our work and the sacred nature of our lives are not dictated by where we are, then wherever we are is holy. We do not need to take a purse or a special tunic on our journey, because the walk itself is sacred; and the gifts and treasures that are holy cannot be bought or sold.

The path of the cleaning woman at the top of the Vatican was sacred not because of its location but because it was a path of service. In the midst of great power and circumstance, surrounded by roads paved with marble and gold, she was the disciple calling me back to the path of humility that is found only in service.

BON AQUA

THERE IS A LITTLE TOWN IN TENNESSEE CALLED BON AQUA—
literally, "good water." I traveled there one day with
friends and found a field where we dreamed of building
a church. We imagined it over a well where you could sit
and pray and look deep into the water. It was a sweet
idea. Then we started wondering where the water was.

One of the men offered to make a divining rod. He cut
two pieces of thick wire, bent them at a ninety-degree
angle, and held them straight out in both hands. Slowly
he began walking across the field; and when he got to a
certain place, the wires turned toward each other.

"There's water here," he said.

"Are you kidding?" I asked, shocked and excited.

"No," he said. "You try it."

Following his instructions, I held the wires loosely in
my hands. When I reached the same spot, the wires
turned toward each other as if drawn by a magnet.

We never did dig for water. If we had, I believe we
would have found it. I believe that because I felt the pull
in my chest. We are made to feel the pull. We can tell
what's under the surface and where the Spirit is living.
As I make my way on the journey, when I feel them pull
I need to dig there and find life-giving water.

THE CHICKEN COMES
BEFORE THE EGG

I HAVE LEARNED OVER THE YEARS THAT ON THE SPIRITUAL journey, the chicken comes before the egg. Before we can start appreciating the great gift of their eggs, we have to spend time getting to love the smelly creatures. They don't use the sense that God gave them—the sense that fits on the head of pin.

Every year when I travel to Ecuador, I have to familiarize myself with chickens again. I have to grow accustomed to their crowing all night and roaming freely in houses and yards. It took about five years for me to walk peacefully among the chickens and not think a bad thought about them.

That fifth year, on my path near the chickens, I came across an old woman who carried her journey on her face. The woman had come to see the doctors. I talked with her while she waited. In front of her, in a line that stretched inside, were translators, guitar players, people playing with the children, and patients. I had noticed the woman for a couple of years, and so it was nice to sit in the midst of the activity and wait with her. I remembered that a couple of years ago she had come to the clinic for tears for her eyes. It was as if she had cried all of hers and so needed the doctor to give her artificial tears. Now, two years later, when she finally sat down with the doctor, I could tell there was a new problem. The doctor called another doctor over; and after consulting together, they explained through a translator that she was seriously ill with a mass in her abdomen. The woman blinked for a minute with no tears and then went on to describe her pain and suffering. Sadly, there was nothing the doctors could do for her. As the woman got up to leave, she asked if I wanted to come with her. "Sure," I said, not realizing she lived a long way off past the curve in the two-line highway and up into a muddy side road.

We started walking, and I was caught off guard by how little there was to say. There I was on the other side of the equator, walking along a dusty path with a dying woman. My vision under the sun felt clear; and I decided right then and there to give up worrying, to live for peace, to forgive everyone, and to sing from my heart. In that moment, not much else would have made sense. We arrived at her cement home and sat in a two-chair room with chickens roaming freely in and out. I was lost in thoughts and prayers for her and for the world that holds so much disparity. Then she got up, gave me a cold drink, and gathered five eggs from the corner, carefully wrapping each one in paper as a present.

Isn't it just like love to take you down such a road? When you begin to feel comfortable with chickens, you get eggs. When you accept death, you are given life. When you think you may be at peace with a dying woman who has no tears, an ocean wells up in you and you taste mercy.

THE EXQUISITE BEAUTY
OF BEING THERE

MANY TIMES, THE EXPERIENCE OF READING A STORY SEEMS flat and inadequate when compared with what it must have been like to witness the words as they were spoken. Just try to imagine what it was like for the people walking with Jesus during his ministry. For three years, the small tribe traveled toward Jerusalem, moving closer to power and danger as their leader continued revealing signs and wonders. They must have spent whole nights discussing and dissecting texts, conversations that surely seemed revolutionary and frightening. They must have felt awed by the charismatic presence of the man who has inspired a world for two thousand years. They must have wondered what was coming as he spoke in beautiful, poetic images. I wonder if there was sadness in the air, even as he talked about joy. I imagine the tension rising as conflicts with the authorities intensified. Jesus, who had given everything of himself to the community, said that he would offer his flesh for the beliefs he had revealed. I can almost imagine it, but there are a thousand images I can't envision because I wasn't there.

Trying to imagine what it was like to be with Jesus is like trying to describe a kiss or telling someone how it

felt to sit at the bedside of your beloved and say goodbye.
Some things do get lost in translation. In order to understand an experience fully, we have to have walked the journey, risked something of ourselves, and allowed it to change us. For example, I have noticed that every now and then, Communion tastes like living bread. I've tried to put the feeling into words, but the description is flat when compared with the experience itself. I can almost describe the way you walk up the aisle a thousand times; and then, on the thousand-and-first time, peace and forgiveness wash over you as the bread melts in your mouth. I can almost describe perfectly how precious it is to stand with a community and, just as the wine warms your throat, you remember someone you loved who has died. I can almost explain how it feels to have hope rise in your chest or to feel love for a stranger. But how can I describe the joy of tasting living bread? If you have never shared in Communion, you can only get a cloudy glimpse of how beautiful and tender it is to see the circle of outstretched hands with palms waiting to be filled. In that moment, there is richness in the silence. Words cannot do justice to it. The best that words can offer is an invitation to experience it.

Mere preaching on sacred texts falls short of conveying their beauty and mystery. Texts must be walked to be understood, and no one can walk them for us. In a life of faith, our texts are heard in the heart. It is living the faith that allows people to walk in peace through a world at war. It is living the gospel that washes the reader in gratitude and love.

Several years ago I helped to open a Magdalene community out of St. Stephens Church in Charleston, South Carolina. As I described Magdalene to the people of that church, I had the problem of trying to explain a faith and having that explanation lost in translation. I watched their newly formed board begin conversations about opening a house that had no live-in staff or rental fees. The board was worried about violence, money, and the effect that Magdalene would have on their church. I could only say that after ten years I am more faithful because at the first five Magdalene houses there has never been one bit of violence, period. I could only say that every time I have worried about money, it has been there. I could only say that I know many women who are now living independently with their families. I could tell that the words fell far short.

What I could not explain was how the experience of sitting in a jail with women has brought home all the injustices of our system and how that fires my heart to work for change. Or how it feels to be on Dickerson Road with women who think you are wasting their time because they could be collecting ten dollars for crack. Or how impossible it is not to scream about sexual abuse and the drug-and-sex industry in the city. What I could not describe was the feeling when, after sitting with a woman for a year, she introduces you to her child, who looks just like her.

Later in Charleston, I had another insight into the difference between reading and living the text. I decided to go to the beach, and while planning the trip I began writing about it. I wrote that I was filled with the anticipation of sitting in sand, where thoughts have more room to wander, where I could hear nothing but wind and waves, where I squinted to see the sea gulls dip near the water. But when I walked out onto the beach at sunrise the next morning, the experience was an ocean better than its advent. I had forgotten the feeling of salt water lapping on my feet. I had forgotten the stillness of a rising sun hanging like Saturn with a band of cirrus clouds cinched around its waist. I had forgotten the exquisite details of the ocean's eternal beauty washing over me. I could not have imagined how the sun cut a rainbow path across emerald waters with diamond insets. I couldn't imagine it or read about it; I had to go and sit and adore it.

Texts are just one of the manifestations of God's love for the world. Texts offer us an invitation to experience for ourselves the joy and tenderness of communion with God. Texts aren't the experience itself; they just invite us in. Texts pale beside the exquisite beauty of being there.

helpful hints

- Remember, the church created the Bible; the Bible didn't create the church.

- Don't confuse access to power with power. A friend and fellow preacher and I met to dream up ideas for launching an anti-war movement. He told me that just because I had friends in power didn't mean I had power myself.

- Learning exactly what Yahweh meant by the words *thou shall not kill* could take a lifetime.

- When you feel you can't pray, go to a temple, mosque, synagogue, or church, because other people will pray for you.

- If you can't practice your religion in the woods, in prison, or at home, you need to change the practice of your religion.

- If people begin to argue a religious or moral belief in a mean-spirited way, suggest that they close their holy book and hit you over the head with it. It's simpler and more straightforward.

A Prayer for Living

Thank you for time to remember your grace
*   and mercy, especially when we are in trouble.*
Thank you for guiding us along the path
*   to make our way to you.*
Remove from our hearts whatever we hold onto
*   that keeps us from moving forward gracefully.*
Please forgive us our doubts.
Give us the energy to tend the gardens we have laid
*   and all for your love's sake.*
Amen.

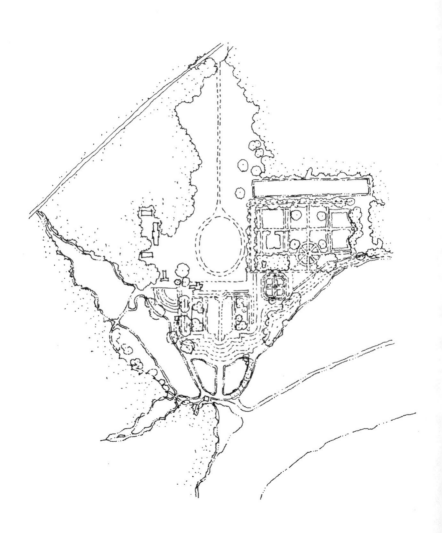

6. traveling to idealism

The Trinity of Moses, Jesus, and Mohammad

Tea glasses toast in old Cairo
As they laugh about the old Pharaoh
Then close in prayer beside the Pyramid
The trinity of Moses, Jesus, and Mohamad

Witnesses to weightless words
And holy books turned into swords
Tired of death in their collective name
And all the outcasts full of shame

For the sake of love they surrender talk
Call the faithful instead to walk
And seek a lost and precious pearl
Along the edges of the world

With no purse or holy book
That you have to defend if someone took
These pilgrims forsake the truth
And look for a balm that can soothe

No one speaks of justice or peace
But walk until the wars cease
The trinity then close their eyes
Their divinity not yet realized

And two by two we come for a sign
So we remember their love is divine
Then they send us out again
Moses, Jesus, and Mohammad

HOPE WAS BORN IN PRISON

IN THE BEST OF WORLDS, OUR THEOLOGY IS NOT AN ARGUMENT to be defined and then defended against contrary thoughts. It is the story of our lives unfolding to express our gratitude for all that God has given us. "God is good" is the best story we can tell, and we can tell it all the time.

One of the most powerful examples I have ever heard of this was on a visit to a woman who had returned to jail. "How are you doing?" I asked, ready for the laundry list of problems she faced legally and financially with her family. "God is good," she said without hesitation. If we believe that God is good, then we have to surrender to that truth wherever we are in our travels. God is good when we get cancer or when we are healed. God is good when we are lost or found. God is good when we live and when we die.

Not long after speaking to the woman in jail, I met with another woman named Hope who had been released from prison and had decided to come into one of our Magdalene houses. Hope was born in prison. After her mother gave birth and before the state took the baby away, her mother had named her Hope. Hope's father was already dead, so Hope became an orphan. She was raised in more than a dozen foster homes and ended up on the streets by the time she was sixteen. Hope was abused as a child and raped as an adult. Hope was battered and almost killed. Hope can sing like an angel. Hope can tell you about dreams that seem impossible from her vantage point. Hope is alive; and even though scarred, she carries her namesake to others by her very presence. Hope is strong and trusts profoundly, not in the fairness of the world but in the steadfastness of God.

Hope is one of the highest ideals to keep us steady on this walk. It is what keeps people praying in prison. Hope gives us rest wherever we are. It assures us that we will be okay, because eventually we are headed home. We can stand firmly on hope; it's not some lofty, ethereal vision that will leave us when times are rough. It is hope that kept early faith communities alive during times of persecution, and it has always been a sign of God's Spirit among us. Hope lives in all of us and carries us forward when we grow weary. Learning to accept that gives us power we have never seen.

LOOKING FOR LOVE

THE SPIRITUAL JOURNEY IS GUIDED BY LOVE, AND SOMETIMES that love is expressed in overwhelming romantic passion. The love that I am talking about is called *eros* in Greek. It is a powerful force that has toppled kingdoms and changed hearts. Part of living into the ideal of hither and yon is to welcome this kind of love, striving for a place where our sexuality and spirituality can live together. We don't have to check our bodies at the door to be in communion with God. We can celebrate that we are spiritual beings in human flesh and can experience love through another human being.

The point is not that we are able to love, for that is how we are made. The work is learning to love faithfully as part of our covenant with God. Loving faithfully means not letting our spiritual and physical selves divide. It is not simply about respecting ourselves and our beliefs. It is not about declaring rules and laws that people use like mortar to build secret rooms. It is about treating the other person as a sacred treasure and honoring that person in body, mind, and spirit. It is about promising to be faithful to the beliefs we hold while loving another.

The religious institutions of the world make honest conversation about this kind of love almost impossible. They tend to establish strict codes for everyone to live by, where in reality only a small percentage of people live out that code. The people who act outside that code feel shame and whisper their fears and secrets. Whenever fear and shame step into the space of love, the tendency toward abuse becomes stronger.

It would be wise to ask seminarians who are heading out into the world, "What are you going to do when you fall in love?" Many spiritual paths veer dramatically when love for another enters the picture. Suddenly people are open to change, have the will to move, are able to hear the Spirit, will consider taking a pilgrimage far away. Family trees have been changed forever by two people whose paths cross and they take that quick, second look. In my own experience, falling in love changed the course of my journey forever. I literally ran into my husband in a divinity school hallway. Within a few months we were talking about getting married, raising children, and making sure we would never be separated. I changed my graduate school plans, changed where I lived, and compromised some of my short-term goals so that we could be together.

What a great gift we have been given to love others in body, mind, and spirit. What an amazing gift to offer it all back to God in gratitude.

A PLACE CALLED GILEAD

THERE IS A REGION SOMEWHERE EAST OF THE JORDON RIVER called Gilead. No one knows exactly where it is, but it is said to heal the sin-sick soul. It is the Promised Land, where we taste milk and honey and know the balm that can soothe our hearts and minds. We have all dreamed of Gilead, and some have had the clouds part in front of their eyes to see visions of it.

I love believing in Gilead. It calms my mind to imagine its shade trees and thick wild flowers growing taller than my head. I imagine it as a new Eden where we enter and mysteriously know our way around. Questions arise about who can enter Gilead and what are the requirements for going there. Somewhere along the way, I have surrendered those questions, not giving much thought to salvation, reincarnation, or karma. I know that access to such a region comes only with God's grace, and that grace is universal. The flowers of Gilead bloom for everyone who cares to glimpse their beauty and take in their fragrance. The trees in Gilead shade anyone who sits under them, with no regard for the person's spiritual condition or past actions.

When we trust the journey to God, we offer God all that we have in this life and pray that we will go well into the next. Several years ago I sat with a man who was dying. He had been unable to speak for several days and was struggling for each breath. His family was sitting around him in prayer, telling him it was okay to die. I imagined him standing on the edge of a great cliff. Everyone was calling up to him, "The water is great, just jump"; but the only person who truly knew how difficult it was to jump was the man standing on the edge. When it was quiet for a minute, I leaned toward him and whispered my goodbye into his ear. I asked him to pray for me when he arrived where he was headed.

It is a great privilege to watch the spirit take the leap and leave the body and to think about the great mystery that is unfolding as we sit and grieve.

THINGS LEFT UNDONE

THE LAW OF THE UNIVERSE IS THAT LOVE NEVER DIES. IT IS written deep in the heart of creation and has been translated in many ways in a multitude of times and places. It is voiced by the prophet, telling us to write this law on the hearts of our children. It is preached by apostles, saying that faith, hope, and love remain when everything else passes. It runs so deeply that people in exile for generations can still dream of love. In all religions, in all times, in all places, love holds humanity in a common bond to God. It calls us to love God with all our hearts and minds and bodies, and to love our brothers and sisters as ourselves. It is obvious when we break this law. We know it. We say we are sorry and try to make amends. Perhaps the hardest thing is to look back on the road and realize what we have left undone.

A few years ago, I was driving to Chattanooga, Tennessee, with a graduate of Magdalene who was moving there to help start a new community. "I don't know if you heard," she said, "but Vicky died." She said it casually, as you might tell an old friend about a mall or a restaurant that had closed. Immediately my mind was flooded with images of Vicky, who smoked like a man and whose body always stayed in shape no matter how hard she abused it. I could see her sitting on my porch, debating with me about God and the criminal justice system. My friend continued, "She overdosed on heroin after they released her from jail." Then it hit me. The last time Vicky was in jail, she had written me a long letter. She had had a conversion experience, but there were loose ends. She wrote out some of her questions and asked me please to write her back. I never did. I thought to myself that this was what the sin of omission feels like. A weight pressed on my chest. If I had been in water, I would have sunk to the bottom. Suddenly I began to remember all the other things I had failed to do. They were out there, just waiting. This one was only the most recent.

As we travel on the journey, the list of things left undone keeps growing. As people die, some of those things will never be done. Now I can never write Vicky a letter or talk with her about God or help her with questions such as why the innocent suffer. Now she is sitting at the right hand of God. All the questions have been laid aside with her needle; and when I throw myself at the mercy of love, Vicky is the one who will offer it to me.

"I didn't write her back," I said to my friend in the car. "That's all right," she said. Then she launched into a great story about Vicky. As she spoke, I could feel the weight lifting as the law of love began to work. Was I forgiving myself, or was Vicky forgiving me? Maybe it didn't matter.

I am sorry, Vicky, that it took me so long to get back to you. Now I have to pray my letter to you; but since love never dies, maybe it's not too late. I suppose there is no longer any reason to answer your questions. Instead, I find myself in the position of needing to ask you some. Can you hear this prayer? Was all the pain of your journey healed in death? Do you forgive everyone? Tell Love I am sorry for all the things done and left undone. The rest I will carry with me as memory on the road.

helpful hints

- Radical love is the foundation for change. Tolerance is the beginning of learning to love radically.

- If you can live without ever worrying about having something taken from you, most of your fears would disappear.

- At times the face of God is as plain as the nose on your face.

- Your cross is not what you are willing to live with; it is what you are willing to die for. Therefore, pick up your cross and follow your bliss—that unbridled joy found on the path to union with God.

- Every Eucharist, maybe for the four hundred ninetieth time, is an invitation to be washed by the miracle of forgiveness.

A Prayer of Hope

Let the sun set in bands of orange and pink.
Let the waves dance in a perfect chorus line.
Let the dandelions scatter confetti seeds
throughout the land.
Let the children's hearts be so full of love
that they cry together.
Amen.

7. endings and beginnings

In the Aftermath

In the aftermath
When shadows are long
Smell and memories linger
While I am figuring

Recalling regrets and blessings
Things done and left undone
That add up to my past

Watching the day spent
Just add length on
To my shadow

Near as I can figure
If all that remains is love
Everything else adds up to nothing
In the aftermath

THE COST OF THE JOURNEY

I MET MY FRIEND DANIELLE FOR LUNCH THE OTHER DAY. I have known her about ten years, and her positive spirit and faithfulness are palpable. I have seen her endure heartbreaks and job stress and still be loyal and hopeful about the next day.

Last year she married the man of her dreams in South Carolina and immediately became pregnant. She was ecstatic that at the age of forty this great fortune had fallen on her. During the pregnancy she discovered her baby, Mera, was not going to live long outside the womb because of a genetic disorder. Danielle decided to carry the baby to term and spent the next few months with her husband preparing for the birth and death of their first-born. She picked out the dress and blanket that would welcome her baby into the world and would be her burial dress. She had cameras ready and a priest on hand for the baptism.

The birth and death took place a month ago, and at lunch she showed me pictures of her beloved daughter. "I'm not angry at God," Danielle said, with eyes brimming. "I just miss having Mera with me." As she recounted the story, I began to think about the cost of love for Danielle. It seemed to set her on a high perch near the heart of God. One way or the other, the cost always consists of laying down our lives for the love of others. It is an enormous cost, but that is what it means to seek the heart of God.

We cannot avoid pain in this world. The choice is between the pain of loving or the pain of not being able to love.

SAYING GOODBYE
TO PEOPLE WE LOVE

No matter who we are, it is hard to say goodbye to people who have traveled with us on this side of eternity. What is important is that we are bound for the Promised Land and union with God. Lauren McCathern, a beautiful student at Belmont University who was battling bipolar disease, killed herself one day in October. I didn't know it then, but it was the beginning of a journey toward learning about resurrection.

Lauren's absence still speaks volumes. It was a holy week when she died, and her death colored the mood of ministry at St. Augustine's Chapel for the next year. The death was raw and startling, because Lauren was a young woman who had welcomed social justice into her theology, had traveled with us on our yearly trip to work at a school in Ecuador, and had chosen to turn toward people who needed her. It was haunting that this peaceful, young woman with a glorious smile could take her life in a violent way. Her death felt like more than death. To me, it epitomized the meaning of tragedy and quiet desperation. It took place in a world weary with war, with mind-numbing poverty, and with devastation from hurricanes and genocide; and somehow my grieving for Lauren included all those things. She embodied suffering innocence. She reminded me that when one suffers, we all suffer. The grief we feel for one connects us to all grief for all times.

In the spring after Lauren's death, a student named Rachael Moody was the recipient of a scholarship given in Lauren's memory, enabling Rachael to travel with us for the first time on our annual trip to Ecuador. She was a translator. Our theme for the journey was signs and symbols. Before we left on the trip, I had emailed the twenty-eight travelers, "Rest in the knowledge that waiting for us outside the school is the almond tree that has been our symbol of hope and faith for ministry." That tree had been a sign of the way good ministry thrives. Each year we had returned, believing that faith and hope would take root and remain long enough to see new growth. But this year, when the bus pulled up to the school, the first thing we saw was the startling image of the dead almond tree. It had been killed by poison at its base.

We spent the next three days thinking about it. On the third night, sitting in the chapel and facing the door that framed the almond tree, Rachael spoke. She said that when we had arrived, she felt that she had come home; and she was planning to come back to teach for the summer. She said she had never imagined that God had a calling for her or that she was worthy, but she knew it was true. Through tears, she said that if she had not met Lauren and been invited to Ecuador, she never would have come. The almond tree was Lauren, and it seemed dead; but coming from a branch was this beautiful young woman speaking of new life.

That moment, even though rooted in death, was filled with faith and hope. Sometimes when we are lost on the journey, we travel to the deadest of the dead spaces and find that love lives. That is what I had forgotten about life with God. It is easy to forget. It is easy to forget when your heart is clouded by grief. It is easy to forget when you are staring at dead trees. On the Good Fridays of our lives, we celebrate Jesus hanging on a dead tree for hours in the crowning act of love. He looked dead. He was dead. His death appeared to be the epitome of all innocent suffering. For the gathered crowd, it must have felt as if faith itself was dead. On my own Good Fridays, it seems that wars will never cease, that AIDS and poverty will wipe out another generation, that everyone will succumb to the streets, and that no one will be left in any of the Magdalene houses. For the disciples, it must have seemed hopeless; and that is why they were huddled in a room, staring at death. Death was real, and it moved Magdalene, Salome, and Mary the mother of James to go to the tomb to care for his dead body.

But Good Friday always leads us back to Easter. Whenever I have forgotten the law of love written in the heart of God, the spirit of that law speaks and says that faith and hope never die.

Faith and hope roll away huge rocks and rise from dead trees, reminding us to quit seeking the dead among the living and to quit seeking the living among the dead. Faith and hope live in death, and love rises to meet them. We will never be dead. There is nowhere that faith cannot grow. There is nowhere that love cannot cut a path and grow hope. We will die and be led back to God.

I am always going to cling to the lesson of the almond tree. There is a place of consciousness on the eternal side of time. We will be filled with faith and hope so that the last stones left in our hearts will be rolled away, and we will be carried to the heart of God.

THE DENOUEMENT

THERE IS A TIME WHEN WE HEAD BACK FROM HITHER AND YON. That time has been described as coming down from the mountaintop or coasting. It is like the pause after a long run, when we sense that we must rest and not push forward. It is the denouement.

In a novel, the denouement comes after the climax of the story. Loose ends are tied, and the reader is taken carefully to the end. Our life journeys also have a denouement. It is a time to relax, reflect, and refresh for the next phase. It is a gift to be experienced with feet kicked up, laughing with friends, or lying neck-deep in a bathtub. It is a place where we allow the details to fade and let the cream rise to the top. In this place, we can glean our lessons and remember how love lives on. To miss the denouement is to forget the graceful glide of a hawk, to overlook the gifts you can find only on Christmas night after everyone has gone home, to neglect the beauty of the line of smoke after a candle is blown out.

The other day I went to the zoo with my youngest son. He wanted to ride the carousel, which was fine by me. Masterfully designed, the carousel is made up of animals that are hand-painted and dedicated to various individuals.

When we got there, my son announced, "I want to ride the dolphin." It was one o'clock on a sunny, 100-degree day; and we were the only people in line. "Please, Mom," he said, "I really want to ride the dolphin. When they open the gate, you go get it for me, and then when I come, let me have it." "Okay, sweetie," I said with all the affection and tenderness of the best moments between mothers and sons. "But there is no one else here. Just walk over to it." "Thanks, Mom," he said.

As the music started and I watched him from the lion's back riding his dolphin, I glimpsed the denouement. I saw not the beauty of the carousel but the magic of a child who maybe for the last time in his life felt the joy of believing he was riding a dolphin, a child who could still wear a cape with dignity and ask "why" questions with no apologies. I loved him like God, completely and eternally, with no thought about the past or future. We were just riding in a circle, going up and down to sweet music. I rarely reach that place of bliss that my son visits regularly; but through the grace of a circle, I came back around and found it for just a minute.

STARTING OVER

ONCE A SERVANT WORKED FOR YEARS ON A BIG ESTATE FOR a just employer. Each day, after tending to the myriad tasks that demanded his time and attention and before he sat in the kitchen to read his paper and eat, the servant would take dinner to his employer. The employer saw this as normal. It never occurred to him to take dinner to the servant. Furthermore, the servant never saw this task as an imposition; it was simply what was expected. He didn't seek praise, because he was just doing his job. Jesus tells this story in the Gospel of Luke. His final line is worthy of an epitaph: "You are servants, and you have done no more than is required of you."

When we have traveled as far as we know how, have given to those in need, have sheltered the homeless, and have loved our neighbor, we have done no more than is required. When we have taken care of the myriad tasks that need tending in our part of the vineyard, we are to keep working without being in need of praise. The next day we are called to head back out and work again.

Once at five in the morning I stood with my mother, the director of a community center, as the center was burning down. She had just completed a capital campaign and the first stages of a renovation that made the horrific fire even sadder. "It looks like arson," the fire chief said as television camera crews arrived and red lights flashed in the morning sky. "Oh, well," my mother sighed as she pulled a pad and pen from her purse. She stood there and began making a to-do list. She never thought that walking away was an option. I never heard her complain about it. I never heard her say she wished for a minute that her life were different. She had raised money and offered service to a community only to have vandals destroy it. Now she would begin again.

THE SPIRIT WILL COME AGAIN

ONCE WHILE WE WERE IN ECUADOR, AFTER WE HAD BEEN working all week in the clinic and traveling, we stopped to have Communion together by the ocean on a beautiful Sunday morning. We were sunburned and tired, but before leaving we gathered by the water's edge in a one-ring circle of endless prayer. As the laughter stilled, the Spirit came from nowhere and the liturgy began. A string of birds, black kites, flew straight over the circle in perfection against a flawless sky. A lone fisherman, searching for new waters with worn nets slung over his thin back, passed by and tipped his hat. Then, as the last of our abundant bread was cast upon the waters, blue-angel pelicans dove in daringly low, skimming the waves. The diamond-filled waters flashed like fireworks, exploding and fading so quickly that it made me feel dizzy. Wonder welled so deeply in my eyes that I saw with kaleidoscope vision. Everything—the water, sand, and faces—danced for an eternal moment.

And then it was over. The curtain came down. Standing in damp sand and laughing with friends, I was left clutching a Bible that contained old and foreign stories, hardly believing the parade that had just passed by.

helpful hints

- Give time to that place between dreaming and being awake. It is sacred ground where new ideas are free to take root.

- Don't grow weary of other people's stories. All war stories have truth in them and teach us something about our own lives. They all deserve a good listener.

- Keep walking on familiar and new paths. The paths are like friends, silver and gold, to be treasured.

- Anoint yourself and make rituals in your daily living. It will help you mark your life as sacred.

- Allow yourself the luxury of grieving your own life when you remember your mortality and the sweetness of a new day.

- Pray for the dead.

- Practice nonviolence.

Closing Prayer

The journey to you, O God, leaves us so tender
    a breeze could break our hearts.
So talk to us in whispers and sweet silence
    until we can walk again.
Be present with us, even as we take our rest.
Then strengthen our desire for courage.

Enkindle our hearts to meet injustice
    in our world and in our thoughts.
Give us tears as a sign of compassion
    for the suffering of the world.
Give us laughter as a sign of joy
    in your wondrous creation.
Thank you for teaching us
    the cost of living in faith and trust.

Teach us to grieve our lives when we need to let go.
You are our God.
Amen.

DISCUSSION AND REFLECTION GUIDE

1. Planning the Journey

It Begins With a Thought

What emotion can you attach to a time when you felt God's presence strongly? What stumbling blocks prevent your returning to that place between head and heart? Can you give yourself permission to imagine, dream, pray, and commune with God from a place within yourself?

Prayer: Ask God for guidance on these next steps of the journey.

The Eternal Timeline

Can you picture yourself standing in the present and eternal moment without looking forward or backward? What issue of injustice speaks to your heart and calls you to a passionate response?

Prayer: Thank God for the eternal moment and the resolve to seek it.

The Map

Do you have markers that outline your spiritual map? When you found yourself, lost yourself, forgot yourself, remembered yourself, and loved yourself, how did God's grace call you back to love? Are there spiritual writings that have led you on your path?

Prayer: Offer a prayer of thanksgiving for markers that have pointed you toward God.

The Legend

What signs have you been given that called you into God's presence to see the world as sacred and to understand how you are a part of creation? Are there specific places, sights, and sounds that evoked your understanding?

Prayer: Pray for the discernment to understand the signs and to love yourself as a unique part of creation.

2. Preparing to Travel

Head Toward the Fear

What fears separate you from love? When have you been able to overcome your fear and find love?

Prayer: Pray that God will empower you to overcome what keeps you from love and to be present with others in their times of fear.

Cleaning House

What can you clean out of your life, literally and metaphorically, that keeps you from being open to the world? What is the one thing you think you can't live without?

Prayer: Ask God to fill your temple with only that which is pleasing in God's sight.

Packing Light

Can you recall a time when you have needed and experienced the generosity of others? Can you imagine what baggage you carry that you can leave behind?

Prayer: Praise God for the blessings of being in need, and ask God for the will to walk unburdened with an open and trusting heart.

What to Wear

Can you laugh about a time in your life when you have worried needlessly? On a scale of one to ten, how important is your clothing?

Prayer: Celebrate that you recognize God wherever you are.

What to Eat

Have you spent much time thinking about the ways God has given you spiritual food that nourishes your journey? Consider fasting and experience how it enables you to be more intentional on your spiritual journey.

Prayer: Rejoice in prayer that you have spiritual food to feed your soul.

Learning the Language

What are your prayers that are grounded in a desire to be with God? Why is the language of prayer such a mystery?

Prayer: Give thanks for the prayers you give and for those offered up for you.

Bread for the Journey

Whatever bread you eat, try to savor it as the embodiment of God in your life.

Prayer: Give God thanks for living bread.

3. Traveling Well

Walking Well-worn Paths

Do you have an internal list of what you might do, read, or reflect on that will fortify you on your journey? Do you practice meditation, contemplation, and prayer daily so that your intention is not forever just a list? Define the moral laws that have been written on your heart, and describe those you wish to add. Do you pray with your closest partners?

Prayer: Ask God to help you persist in your practice so that when you are called upon, you can dance.

Listening to the Birds

Which bird speaks to you in the middle of the day if you hear her song? When others seek you out, can you just listen and not break the silence?

Prayer: Thank God for the wonders of creation and for the powerful lesson found in listening.

Walking in the Woods

Can you imagine a spiritual life without some communion with nature? What is your favorite tree?

Prayer: Give God thanks the next time you pass a chorus of wildflowers.

Traveling on the Fringes
How would you describe the fringes of your life? Do you believe that people choose to live on the fringes? How do you reconcile the suffering of the innocent with an all-loving God?

Prayer: Offer a prayer for those who will follow you, that they may dance on the fringes.

Taking Right Action
How do you know the right path? Has God spoken to you, and if so how did you respond? Are you willing to act with the knowledge that your faith may cost you something?

Prayer: Ask God for the discernment to know the path and the courage to walk on it.

4. Persevering

Keep Walking Until the Bad Spirits Get Bored
Do you know who is beating the drums of your heart? Have you stopped to listen to those drums, reminding yourself that every moment is a part of your dance?

Prayer: Ask God for the perseverance to keep moving until the dance is over and all that remains is love. Pray that God helps you continue to believe when you have grown tired.

The Journey Isn't Fair
Can you think of ways to stop begrudging things to others and complaining that the world is unfair? How can your faith play a role in beginning to see the image of God in everyone?

Prayer: Stand before God in a prayer of gratitude for a world that is not fair.

Walk Farther Than You Meant
Reflect on a time when you were afraid to leave your sea of calm but did anyway, risking all. How did your faith compel you to go deeper? How is your faith calling you to do what your fear keeps you from doing?

Prayer: Petition God for the faith to overcome your fears.

When Bad Things Happen on the Way
Do you allow others to share your pain by telling them your story? How can you honor another's path?

Prayer: Thank God for the universe in which all ground is sacred.

Can't See the Spider for God
On your journey, what is the path that leads you to see God? What causes you to lose sight of the path and prohibits you from seeing God in all creation?

Prayer: Give God thanks for beauty and for the eyes to behold God in everything.

To Hell and Back
Describe a time when you have experienced hell. What made it possible for you to continue your journey? Were you able to continue out of gratitude and without judgment?

Prayer: Ask God to turn your life over to love.

5. Stories for the Road

Coincidences

When in your life has an apparent coincidence been revealed as a pattern in God's mercy and allowed you to be at peace? Are you able to accept God's mercy and love in your life?

Prayer: Ask for strength, for the courage to be aware of God's presence, and for the fortitude to continue.

A Coptic Church in Old Cairo

Imagine yourself removing the nails from the feet of Christ. What are some ways in which you can honor the work of the Lord by preserving the works of others? Can you set aside your own needs?

Prayer: Ask God to help you be aware of cobwebs and to be humbled by their presence.

The Bathroom at the Vatican

How hard it is to see everything as sacred? When has your perception been clouded by grandeur?

Prayer: Offer a prayer that serving the humblest of your brothers and sisters takes your breath away and leads you to peace.

Bon Aqua

When in your life have you felt the pull in your chest of the divine? How have you responded, and what did you discover? Can you trust in the Spirit, that when you loosen your grip you will be divinely led?

Prayer: Ask God to direct your daily journey and to help you be still so that you may feel the Spirit within.

The Chicken Comes Before the Egg

Can you remember a time when you were given a gift so unexpectedly that it mirrored the gift of the five eggs? How can faith give you the strength to accept life's disparity?

Prayer: Ask God for the grace to give up worrying, to live for peace, to forgive everyone, and to sing from your heart.

The Exquisite Beauty of Being There

Can you recall a time when you witnessed a vivid manifestation of the Word—a virtual washing of Christ's feet, a feeding of his sheep, a surrendering of self?

Prayer: Ask God that you will accept the invitation to the mystical experience of Communion.

6. Traveling to Idealism

Hope Was Born in Prison

How does your life reflect gratitude for all God has given you? Where has hope held you steadfast in the face of adversity? When has the hope of another been a sign of God's Spirit among us?

Prayer: Ask to fortify your belief that for God nothing is impossible.

Looking for Love

How has love changed the course of your life? In what ways does your religious belief encourage you to embrace the physical and spiritual self?

Prayer: Thank God for the gift of love.

A Place Called Gilead

What allows you to trust your journey to God and allows you to live in Gilead now? What could strengthen your trust so that at the end of your life, you can make the leap fearlessly?

Prayer: Offer to God all that you have in this life, and give thanks for the gift of grace. Ask God to allow you to see the paradise of this world and to give you a heart full of gratitude.

Things Left Undone

Reflect on those things that you have left undone and on those that can never be done. How are you forgiven? Can you offer others the same love that God offers you?

Prayer: Thank God for a forgiveness so great that God gave his only Son to die for you.

7. Endings and Beginnings

The Cost of the Journey
Have there been times in your life when joy and grief came at the same time or in the same events? Are there ways in which joy and grief always go together?

Prayer: Thank God for the ability to experience the entire range of human emotions, and ask for guidance in learning and growing from those experiences.

Saying Goodbye to People We Love
Think about a time when faith itself seemed dead. What led you back to a place of hope? When the daily news reports speak of the suffering of innocents, what rolls away the stones from your heart and leads you to a fuller understanding of the Resurrection?

Prayer: Ask God to give you eyes to see the signs of love that surround you even in suffering and death.

The Denouement
How have you come to experiences of denouement that have led to the rekindling of your spirit? Recall one of those times vividly.

Prayer: Offer thanksgiving to God for the lessons we learn when we coast after our loose ends have been tied.

Starting Over

What would you like to have written as your epitaph? Have you responded to God's call so that your service will honor God's sacrifice?

Prayer: Thank God for the grace that allows you to embrace each day with the Rule of St. Benedict: "Always we begin again."

The Spirit Will Come Again

Can you think of times other than at the Eucharistic feast when the Spirit awakens you to become one body and one Spirit with God? How can you answer the call and fulfill your longing to remain on your journey to Hither and Yon?

Prayer: Ask God to awaken you to the Spirit within, the Spirit that will continue to guide you on your path.

Becca Stevens is an Episcopal priest at St. Augustine's Chapel on the Vanderbilt University campus. She is the founder of Magdalene, a residential community for women with a criminal history of prostitution and drug abuse, and the author of *Finding Balance: A Sisters Bible Study* and *Sanctuary: Unexpected Places Where God Found Me,* nominated by *Christianity Today* as best spirituality book of 2005.

INTERVIEW

An interview with Becca Stevens, founder of Magdalene, a residential community for women with criminal histories of drug abuse and prostitution.

How did Magdalene begin?

In 1997, we opened up a community called Magdalene. And the idea was that it would be a small community for a few women who have had a really rough time—who have had criminal histories of drug abuse and prostitution. These are women who have trouble working through institutional systems, school systems, family systems. Systems have not been kind to them. And the idea was literally to lavish them with love and give them a safe place to live for a couple of years where they could really heal. There would be no authority figure, no live-in staff, no rigid way to be. We invited five women to come in—women who all had at least a ten-year history on the street and a hundred arrests on their records—so it wasn't like they had a lot of other choices or places to go. And we raised the money so they could live together and work on their recovery and work on their spiritual life and be together. And it was the most beautiful experiment I've ever been a part of. The women came and they stayed clean and sober, and all of us were changed in the process.

Why do you think the Magdalene model worked?

Community had a lot to do with it. None of the women had ended up on the streets alone; it had taken a whole community to get there. So it was going to take a community to bring them in. We didn't take any government or state money. This was really about the community giving in gratitude to the women, offering everything for free. The women came and lived in the program, and everything was given to them. And the idea was that whatever you get from us, just give it back to somebody else. And that's been the model, and it's worked that way for years.

Tell us about Thistle Farms.

Each year Magdalene opened up another house until we had four residences. And what we realized was that women were getting clean and sober and were having powerful experiences in community. But economically they were still very, very vulnerable; and they would go back to old relationships that were dangerous, or they would take jobs that put them in harm's way. We wanted to give them a safe work environment where they could get something on their resume and learn how to work and still have that sense of community. So we started Thistle Farms, a cottage industry run by and for the women of Magdalene. It was no accident that we decided to make bath and body care products. The idea is that the products heal your body, and you're offering those products to others to heal their bodies. We believe that in the eyes of God it doesn't matter who's the giver or receiver but that love is present in the exchange. It's like a quilting circle. You know, you can imagine women sitting around and telling their stories and sharing their joys and sorrows; but instead of making a quilt we're making bath and body care products.

What have you learned from Magdalene?

All of us need community. All of us need sanctuary—safe places to go to be ourselves, to be heard and not judged. And in being heard, somehow there's healing. It's not just that you're healing me. It's that in telling you the story, I find God's healing. We've witnessed it for a decade now, being a part of this work. And that is the truth of my life. What I'm the most grateful for in my ministry is my communal experiences in Magdalene. I'm more faithful than when I started out. I'm more hopeful about women and about recovery and about community and about how generous a community can be. We have never, ever gone without. As I said, we are completely dependent on the generosity of others, and it's always been there. And that's a beautiful, beautiful testimony to how powerful community can be.

Learn more about the work of Magdalene and Thistle Farms at *www.thistlefarms.org*.